Working Your Way into Heaven

Stefan Cardinal Wyszynski

Working
Your Way into Heaven

How to Make Work, Stress, and
Drudgery a Means to Your Sanctity

SOPHIA INSTITUTE PRESS®
Manchester, New Hampshire

Working Your Way into Heaven was originally published in Polish as *Duch Pracy Ludzkiej* in 1946. An English translation by J. Ardle McArdle was published under the title *Work* by Scepter Publishers, Ltd., Dublin, and Scepter Press, Chicago, in 1960. In 1995, with the kind permission of the Primatial Institute of Stefan Cardinal Wyszynski in Warsaw, Poland, Sophia Institute Press published an edition entitled *All You Who Labor: Work and the Sanctification of Daily Life*, which was based on the 1960 Scepter Press translation, with some editorial revisions and improvements in the translation. This retitled 1998 edition by Sophia Institute Press is a reprint of the 1995 edition.

Jacket design by John L. Barger

The cover painting is a detail of *The Forge of Vulcan*, by Diego Rodriguez Velasquez, Museo del Prado, Madrid, Spain (Scala/Art Resource, New York).

Sophia Institute Press®
Box 5284, Manchester, NH 03108
1-800-888-9344

Library of Congress Cataloging-in-Publication Data

Wyszynski, Stefan, 1901-
[Duch pracy ludzkiej. English]
Working your way into heaven : how to make work, stress, and drudgery a means to your sanctity / Stefan Cardinal Wyszynski.
p. cm.
Includes bibliographical references.
ISBN 0-918477-73-5 (pbk.)
1. Work. I. Title.
[BJ1498.W913 1998]
261.8'5 — dc21 98-13873 CIP

98 99 00 01 02 10 9 8 7 6 5 4 3 2 1

Table of Contents

Foreword vii

Preface ix

Introduction 3

1. The Problem of Work Today 5
2. The Image of God's "Work" 13
3. Work as a Need of Human Nature 23
4. Work as a Social Duty 31
5. The Use of the Fruits of Work 41
6. Human Work as Cooperation with God 49
7. Work as Love for the Creator 59
8. Prayer through Work 69
9. The Supernatural Organization of Work 79
10. By the Sweat of Your Brow 87
11. The Mystery of Redemption in Work 95
12. The Interior Life and Excessive Work 103
13. The Spiritual and Social Values of Work 111
14. Patience in Work 119
15. The Virtue of Longanimity in Work 127
16. Perseverance and Constancy in Work 137
17. Conscientiousness and Diligence 143
18. Silence in Work 151
19. Cooperation 161
20. Time for Work and Time for Rest 167
21. Sunday 177
22. Joy in Work 183

Biographical Note 189

Editor's Note: The biblical references in the following pages are based on the Douay-Rheims edition of the Old and New Testaments. Quotations from the Psalms and some of the historical books of the Bible have been cross-referenced with the differing names and enumeration in the Revised Standard Version using the following symbol: (RSV =).

Foreword

In the years before *Solidarity* appeared on the scene, Stefan Cardinal Wyszynski, the spiritual leader of Poland, showed us in his pastoral teaching the noble character of work and taught us how to understand our dignity as workers. Then, when we launched our struggle against Communism, his fatherly wisdom inspired us and gave us strength to overcome the great sufferings we endured. Today his teachings continue to guide us and enrich our daily efforts to build a strong and just society.

Working Your Way into Heaven should be read by all those who labor, regardless of their place in society. Reading this book will lighten your daily burdens and give deeper meaning to your life.

Lech Walesa
President of Poland
Founder of *Solidarity*
January 1995

Preface

It is with great joy that I welcome the announcement that Sophia Institute Press is publishing the work of His Eminence Stefan Cardinal Wyszynski entitled *Working Your Way into Heaven: How to Make Work, Stress, and Drudgery a Means to Your Sanctity.*

Working Your Way into Heaven has not lost any of its value for the working person even though it is almost fifty years since the publication of the first edition in 1946.

Human work always requires an understanding of its essential values. Work is neither a curse nor solely a source of material good. Work is a gift of God, an ennobling of the human person, a form of man's cooperation with the Creator, and a kind of social service. Work must ennoble not only what is material, but as Cardinal Wyszynski teaches in *Working Your Way into Heaven,* work must also ennoble the person who works, so that he does not feel denigrated or cheated by the work he does.

Cardinal Wyszynski's stature and his profoundly holy understanding of reality was a great treasure not only for the Church and for our country, but also for the whole human family.

From the depth of my heart I pray that the reading of *Working Your Way into Heaven* will restore in all of its readers a sense of the meaning and dignity of daily difficulties and of individual and social efforts in the realm of work. May God bless you!

Jozef Cardinal Glemp
Primate of Poland
December 1994

Working Your Way into Heaven

Introduction

The endless hardship of work links man's most precious faculties — his physical strength and spiritual powers — in an indissoluble union. In submission to the laws of private life and social life we devote the greater part of our lives to work. We are convinced that human work, although a burden, is our need, our joy, and a great blessing for humanity. Therefore we take on ourselves the task of work in a spirit of complete acceptance.

Such an attitude does not protect us, however, from the physical and spiritual sufferings connected with work. Yet it is possible to diminish them to a considerable degree and to increase the educational meaning of human work, both in the personal and in the social field. Through this, human work will reveal its real aspect more fully, whether this be the moral, religious, cultural, social, or economic aspect. If these pages bring this about, even to some extent, they will be one more proof of the value of work.

1

The Problem of Work Today

The aim of this collection of thoughts is to introduce the Catholic approach to the role of work in human life. Discussions concerning work are nothing new, and much that is very praiseworthy has been said on the subject. We do not claim to say anything better, or even anything new. But the contemporary problem of work is at the very forefront of many important matters, and when we speak of it here we have to take new tendencies and new needs into consideration.

As we see it, it is of considerable importance for the whole of Catholic religious, moral, and ascetic life that there should be a right understanding of work itself and of the role it plays in human life — not merely the personal role, but the social one; not merely the economic role, but the religious one as well. And the aim of understanding all this is to achieve a real integration of work (which is a part of our life) into the fullness of that life, so that work is no longer something cut off from the rest but is something that forms a harmonious whole with it.

The Catholic view of work is not understood

We can see that there are a great many misunderstandings and mistaken views of the question. Those who love and exalt work, those who see it as the greatest social force or even the highest aim in human life, often have reservations about the Catholic attitude. Catholics are felt to be less efficient. Catholic nations are out of the running when it comes to the competition for work; they need the example of non-Catholic, Protestant, Calvinist, or Communist countries,[1] whose different approaches to work have helped them to achieve great prosperity. We have no wish to argue the point here. Instead, we would like to throw some light on the more important principles of the Catholic approach to work. Whatever truth there may be in the opinions we express will then become self-evident.

Christ's parable illuminates the Catholic view

In the Gospel according to St. Matthew, Christ's parable of the laborers who were sent into the vineyard often seems to us somewhat perplexing.

A householder comes to a marketplace several times during the day, and when he sees men standing there idly, he asks them, "How is it that you are standing here, and have done nothing all the day?" Their answer, "Because nobody has hired us," does not reassure him. "Away with you to the vineyard like the rest."[2] This is the solution to the problem. Did the householder need these men? Obviously not: otherwise he would have employed them

[1] These lines were obviously written before the recent economic collapse of Communism — ED.

[2] Matt. 20:1-7.

from the morning onwards and not put himself to the expense of paying a full day's wage for barely an hour's work.

No, the householder is concerned about something quite different: that no one should live without work. We feel, as it were, a reproach in the query "How is it that you are standing here, and have done nothing all the day?"

But those poor unemployed fellows of a bygone day were at once absolved in the householder's eyes: nobody had hired them, although they had come to the marketplace and stood there patiently all day, waiting for work. How old this problem of unemployment is!

There is something more in Christ's parable, however. The question is significant not only in relation to "those who are doing nothing." It is an exhortation to all who govern human beings not to pass by the unemployed indifferently, not to ignore those who do not know how to organize their work, or who have no chance to work, or no will for it. The householder of the Gospel solves this problem: he hires the unemployed men, encourages their labor, organizes it, and pays them their wages.

It is by no accident that this parable of the laborers in the vineyard should be in the Gospel and that, to this day, it should be proclaimed throughout the world. We must see in all this the will of the Holy Spirit. Indeed, how many of Christ's important sermons and deeds have not come down to us? Both the householder's question and the answer to it must have a special meaning for all ages and for the whole world.

This is quite true. The question "How is it that you are standing here, and have done nothing all the day?" is one that recurs with unmistakable insistence. It is repeated even in our own day, but in a new form.

Before World War II we experienced a wave of unemployment. Almost every marketplace in every town, large or small, reminded us of the Gospel scene, except that there were no owners of vineyards. For the great bulk of the people there was not enough work to go around. Unemployment became an occupation. Millions of people on earth showed the will to work, but there was no work for them. Everyone felt that there was something gravely amiss with this state of affairs. Besides the anguished aimlessness of their existence, many of the unemployed endured the scourge of reproach: "How is it that you are standing here, and have done nothing all the day?" Perhaps these reproaches came from the unheeding owners of vineyards?

Christ's question is asked today of those who have no pressing need to work, since they possess accumulated wealth. They, too, are told that they have nonetheless a duty to work. They are reminded in a simplified form of St. Paul's statement "He that does not work, neither let him eat."[3]

There is a certain natural aptness about this judgment, applied to people who do perhaps perform some type of work, but one not easily perceived by society, not very useful, or without very much to justify it.

Under the influence of materialistic thought, cultural, religious, and contemplative work is regarded as having no value. People who work in these areas are asked the question "How is it you are standing here, and have done nothing all the day?" Sometimes it even comes in the form of a reproach: "While we are toiling by the sweat of our brows, they are leading an idle life, exploiting the fruits of our work."

This question is posed quite often today in connection with people given to prayer, interior life, and contemplation. To the extent that the world is preoccupied with work (that is, excessively concerned with one aspect alone, insofar as it overestimates

3 2 Thess. 3:10.

physical work, and does not do justice to spiritual or mental work), this question affects more and more people who are suspected of living off others.

Many people do not consider contemplation and other mental occupations as work at all. Religious orders are recognized only if they are social, educational, or active, while contemplative orders are regarded as social parasites.

Work has recently grown in importance

The Gospel question has a special meaning today in light of the steady growth in the importance of work. And the value of work, in human eyes, increases as its fruits become more obvious. People are working more and more, and doing so in a more planned and systematic fashion.

Far fewer people now work in isolation, consulting their own wishes. Far more now work in an organized, communal manner, dependent on society; and as a result, the fruits of work are becoming increasingly valuable.

All around us we see the fruits, the evidence, of work. It is changing the face of the earth — changing people and their whole appearance. The land is gradually taking on a new aspect; it does not look now as it did a hundred years ago, still less as it looked a thousand or two thousand years ago. We need only compare the uncultivated African jungle with Holland, where even the ocean has been driven from the country, and the floor of the sea made fertile. Human work makes the land more human and closer to God, more responsive to His thought. Wherever we look, everything is the fruit of some work. If we take even the smallest sector of life, we see how progress has come through work.

This very progress opens up new fields of activity. The job that we have already done makes the next one possible and makes its performance easier. The further we proceed with it, the quicker, the more skillful, fruitful, and useful it becomes. We work more but we do it with greater ease.

People are beginning to realize that work is not only a personal matter but that it is a social force. In the past it was said, "Let each one do in his own sphere what the Spirit of God bids him to do; the whole will see to itself." But today people want to "see to" the whole themselves; they do not want to leave its destiny to an unknown, blind force. They want to consolidate and organize the work of the whole community.

The importance of a sound understanding of work

We are so much more a part of society in our work, and so much less our own property. Whether we work and what we do, therefore, is not an indifferent matter. Each individual's strength and ability to work is becoming more and more a social force. It is because of this that the contemporary controversy about the status of work in the world (that is, the controversy about whether work is a purely personal or a social affair) takes place.

Originally this controversy had a moral-religious significance. The Church led the struggle, condemning laziness and idleness in the Pauline verdict "If any man will not work, neither let him eat." Work was numbered among the virtues, while sloth was branded as a sin — and a deadly sin.

Today people, who at one time did not recognize the Church's teaching concerning work, talk about it even more than She does, although from a completely different point of view. Some people recognize only mental activity, which organizes all other forms of labor, and reduce physical work to an executive, mechanical, and supplementary role. Others, on the other hand, slight mental work and extol the physical.

Theories arise proclaiming that work is something important, that it binds everyone, that a state ought to compel everyone to work, that the only person who has any right to life in the state is the worker, that anyone who is unable to work may not have sustenance, that he has no right to anything and ought to be rejected as useless. There even have arisen whole state organizations for the promotion of work.

All of this clearly shows how contemporary, important, and timely is the problem of work. Therefore it is important to determine its essence, character, meaning, and aims so that we are not carried away by mistaken views, so that we might acknowledge the place of work in our lives, and so that we might use work as a means of attaining our end, both temporal and eternal, in life.

2

The Image of God's "Work"

In order to answer the question "What is human work?" it is necessary to consider both God's thought and human life. However, before we enter the temple of work, we must survey it from different angles.

For example, Holy Scripture contains many beautiful thoughts about work. It especially honors the "work" of God Himself. Yet, can one speak of God's work?

The Son of God spoke of it: "My Father has never ceased working, and I, too must be at work."[4] The Son knows what the Father does. And, what is more, the Son justifies His own work by the Father's example.

The very beginning of Revelation sets us face-to-face with God's work. The book of Genesis represents in six images the whole creation of the world, bringing into prominence the indefatigable activity of God. God is the beginning of all activity, of all movement, and of all work. God's "Let there be" contains in itself

[4] John 5:17.

creative thought and achievement at the same time. From this first motion starts all the movement without which man could accomplish nothing.

God conceived the world from all eternity and became the beginning and end of all being and all activity. From this, everything whatsoever moves, lives, grows, develops, and acts, all by means of power drawn from God. To speak the language of our age, the whole world, with all its phenomena and elements, with all the forces that are revealed to us, is all linked to God by conveyer belts, as it were, along which God's power and strength flow from Him to us.

Everything in the universe acts by God's power. If God were to deny His power to the world, even for an instant, it would all be plunged into lifelessness and the shadow of death.

Scripture praises God's work

In words familiar to us all, Psalm 103 makes these thoughts more beautifully vivid by its praise of God's work in the universe. They bring a special clarity into our feelings in the celebration of Pentecost. The whole world has its continual descent of the Holy Spirit, by which the seven gifts flow down to this earth, keeping it in existence, alive, and active.

> *O Lord my God, Thou art exceedingly great.*
> *Thou hast put on praise and beauty:*
> *And art clothed with light as with a garment.*
> *Who stretchest out the heavens like a pavilion*
> *Who coverest the higher rooms thereof with water.*
> *Who makest the clouds Thy chariot*
> *Who walkest upon the wings of the winds.*

Who makest Thy angels spirits
And Thy ministers a burning fire.[5]

God is marvelous in what He does, in the works of His hands, and powerful in the forces at His disposal, creating them to His own use for the execution of His plans.

Who hast founded the earth upon its own bases:
It shall not be moved for ever and ever.[6]

All God's works are exact and perfect; when He builds something, it lasts through the ages.

The deep like a garment is its clothing:
Above the mountains shall the waters stand;
At Thy rebuke they shall flee:
At the voice of Thy thunder they shall fear.
The mountains ascend, and the plains descend
Into the place which Thou hast founded for them.
Thou hast set a bound which they shall not pass over;
Neither shall they return to cover the earth.[7]

It is God's mighty power that raises the peaks of the mountains up out of the heart of the earth, covering them with His glory. It is God by the power of His will who carves out the valleys and mountain crevices, who spreads out the fertile fields like carpets, snatches the waters of the sea up to the heavens and rains them as dew onto the harvests of the earth. It is God's thought that forms the face of the earth in a wonderful way, ornamenting it with the flashes of His beauty.

[5] Ps. 103:1-4 (RSV = Ps. 104:1-4).
[6] Ps. 103:5 (RSV = Ps. 104:5).
[7] Ps. 103:6-9 (RSV = Ps. 104:6-9).

Thou sendest forth springs in the vales:
Between the midst of the hills the waters shall pass.
All the beasts of the field shall drink:
The wild asses shall quench their thirst.
Over them the birds of the air shall dwell:
From the midst of the rocks
They shall give forth their voices.
Thou waterest the hills from the upper rooms.
The earth shall be filled with the fruit of Thy works,
Bringing forth grass for cattle
And grain for the service of men,
That Thou mayst bring bread out of the earth.[8]

Man is God's co-worker

God exercises control over the earth. He establishes the laws of the world. According to these laws everything takes its life from the work of His own hands. God confers on the earth a strange power, which supplies food for the beasts, and produces bread for man. This is the great mystery of the earth, which no agronomic knowledge created, even though it profits from it.

All expect of Thee that Thou shalt
give them food in season.
What Thou givest to them they shall gather up:
When Thou openest Thy hand,
they shall all be filled with gold.
But if Thou turnest away Thy face,
they shall be troubled:
Thou shalt take away their breath,

[8] Ps. 103:10-14 (RSV = Ps. 104:10-14).

and they shall fail,
And shall return to their dust.
Thou shalt send forth Thy spirit,
and they shall be created:
And Thou shalt renew the face of the earth.[9]

This is the picture of the great, farsighted, conscientious, and loving work of God. Everything that lives is bound up with this work; everything is dependent on it for existence. It is worthwhile keeping this picture before one's eyes so as not to overestimate the fruits of one's own work. Man creates nothing; he merely transforms God's ready-made gifts. God alone acts and creates in the true meaning of that word: man is but God's co-worker, His helpmate.

It is God who creates the conditions for our work. Our work would not have any starting point or basis if God did not prepare gifts from which we draw the material for new work. Even today in our technological age, we see how dependent our work is on God's work and activity, further proof of the Savior's words: "My Father has never ceased working."

God, exercising His Providence over the world, designs the whole plan down to the minutest detail; He Himself enacts directly not only the general laws by which the world is to be ruled, but also their smallest subsections. He is concerned for the birds of the air and for every hair on our heads. Yet He entrusts the details of His design to man, to a rational being who, with the help of prudence, must play his part in bringing all creation to the fulfilment of the whole plan intended by God. With this aim God prepared man for the role of His co-worker, endowing him with a rational will able to recognize and carry out God's intentions. God

[9] Ps. 103:27-30 (RSV = Ps. 104:27-30).

showed him the aim of work and gave him strong incentives toward it.

Christ was Himself a worker

But God left the strongest motive in the example of His Son, Jesus Christ, whom He sent into the world in order to fulfil the Father's will and to give us a model of obedience to God. Jesus united His action to the action of the Father. "My Father has never ceased working, and I too must be at work." He describes the Father's work more closely, by calling Him a householder, sower, and husbandman.

The Son of such a hardworking Father, sharing the same nature with Him, also finds in the Father the power to act. As a man, with eyes fixed on God's example, He is drawn into His Father's work. Indeed, the Gospels are silent about the details of Christ's life from the time of His return from the Temple in Jerusalem — where He so boldly began to go about His Father's "work"[10] — until His Baptism. But in one way they reveal to us the mystery of this period. This mystery is that Christ gave many years of His life to physical work.

Public opinion calls Christ an artisan and the son of an artisan. As the supposed son of Joseph, following the example of His foster-father, He practiced His trade and small farming, too. For it was the custom in the Holy Land of those days for every small artisan to supplement his income by cultivating a small plot of ground from which he derived the most basic means of life. Christ in His life saw the labor of artisans and farmers at very close quarters. He took on Himself all the duties of the everyday work that He carried on in His workshop and in the fields.

[10] Luke 2:49.

All of Jesus' teaching bears witness to this. He has a wonderful knowledge of the fields, not from observation but from direct contact with it. He certainly put His hand to the plow more than once, or broke up the rocky ground with the mattock. At times He went out as a sower, and saw that the seed thrown from His hand fell now on rock, now among thorns, now on the roadside, and now on good ground, and that it brought forth varying crops. Indeed, work in the vineyard was not strange to Jesus either. Does He not talk of grafting the vine shoot, of pruning, of dunging? He speaks of the winepress, of the tower, stewards, and night watches. These Gospel parables are too close to real life to have come from the lips of a man who had not had direct experience of their subject. Spending all His time among people at work, Jesus had a thorough knowledge of it and a great respect for it.

For years there has been talk of creating a feast of Christ the Worker. There would be nothing artificial or exaggerated in this. On the contrary, nothing could be nearer the reality. Such a feast would only honor that great labor through which Christ, by His example, taught people to work.

Christ's Apostles were also workers

Christ selected people from the same environment of ordinary, everyday hard work, to labor in the field of His own harvest. He had to have people well used to effort, toil, wearisome sweat, and struggle.

Almost all the Apostles were fishermen, a race of brave men, seasoned in the struggle with the sea, water, and winds, accustomed to nightly vigils. Lake Gennesaret was the school for the Apostles. There, in Peter's boat, they became familiar with apostolic ways on the wide seas of work. That boat would change into the Vatican barque, and Peter into its helmsman.

Agitated waves, a storm at sea, long centuries of struggle and persecutions: what is new in this for God's fishermen and their successors? Only the setting has changed, nothing more. The Church is God's boat in which the hardened, robust, fearless fishermen withstand the violent winds.

The heavenly Workman, the Workman's son Jesus, the disciples, who are fishermen: this is a close-knit family, and one that possesses the old traditions of work. In such surroundings the Christian idea of work first sprang up.

Anyone who has really experienced the taste and burden of work, cannot hold it in contempt. And therefore the Catholic Church has always brought a new spirit into the life and surroundings of human work.

It is well known that, after His Resurrection, Jesus found His disciples at work. They returned to it in the most matter-of-fact way in the world. It never even entered their heads to do anything but go back to their fishing. They were too fond of it; it was in their blood. And so the disciples turned to work to find there some comfort for their pain after the loss of the Master.

The Church has always honored work and workers

From such work Christ also summoned the Apostles to work in the Church. "Henceforth, thou shalt be a fisher of men."[11] This direct link between physical and apostolic work was the starting point for the admiration in which work was held in all Christian thought. This was indeed a clean break with pagan tradition, then all-powerful!

Christ's disciples did not wholly sunder their connection with work. St. Paul is an example of this. Although he knew that "those

[11] Matt. 4:19.

who do the temple's work live on the temple's revenues,"[12] he did not want to burden the poor believers of the first Christian communities, but supported himself, earning his bread by manual labor. And he repeatedly emphasized the duty of work: "Let him work instead, and earn by his own labor the blessings he will be able to share with those who are in need."[13] In the Christian tradition stress is also laid on this new practice (that is, working so as to have means to give to the poor).

The pagans despised every kind of work, even artistic work. They regarded physical work as unworthy of man. It was the duty of slaves. It could not be reconciled with the sublimity of the free mind, for it limited it too much, and made it dependent both on itself and on others.

The pagans said that physical work is harmful because it hurts the body; a really superior man cannot submit to the compulsion of labor, which is opposed to the harmony and beauty of the human body. The pagans thought that the deleterious effects of physical work on the body must have a bad influence on the human spirit.

Christianity did away with this error as well. It brought about the real liberation and elevation of human work. The first Christians, even the rich ones, sometimes showed their membership in the Church by doing physical work. They professed Christ not only in word but in deed. For is it not true that "faith without deeds to show has no life in it"?[14] This attitude conquered the dislike the pagan world had for any sort of work.

What is more, the Christian world emphasized the importance of uniting spiritual and physical work. We see this especially in

[12] 1 Cor. 9:13.

[13] Eph. 4:28.

[14] James 2:17.

monastic life, where the most sublime contemplation has gone hand in hand with manual labor.

Christianity prepared the soil for further social reforms in the sphere of work. It brought about the elevation of work. Now that work is often regarded as a sad necessity to be gotten through for the sake of earning a living, Christianity continues to link it with God. From this linkage flows the whole blessing of work. "For thou shalt eat the labors of thy hands: blessed art thou, and it shall be well with thee."[15]

[15] Ps. 127:2 (RSV = Ps. 128:2).

3

Work as a Need of Human Nature

In Psalm 103 the inspired Author made two laws clear: the law of night and the law of day. The law of the night is "Thou hast appointed darkness and it is night: in it shall all the beasts of the woods go about. . . . seeking their meat from God."[16] The law of day is "Man shall go forth to his work, and to his labor until the evening."[17] The law of day — this is the law of man's work. The animal world retires to its dens and leaves the field open to rational beings. This is man's invitation to work, and the creation of suitable working conditions for him. The law of day is, at the same time, the duty of the day.

Work is the duty of man. This duty arises from the very needs of man's life, as well as from the meaning that work holds for his perfection.

Without work it is not possible either to sustain life or to reach the full development of one's personality. Work is the means of

[16] Ps. 103:20-21 (RSV = Ps. 104:20-21).

[17] Ps. 103:23 (RSV = Ps. 104:23).

sustaining God's gift, life, in us, of properly satisfying its needs, and of perfecting our rational nature.

Man was intended to work even in Paradise

If we reach with our thoughts back into the forgotten time when God declared to man the founding principles of his life, we confirm that from the very beginning it was bound up with the duty of work.

God set man down in Paradise and commanded him "to dress it, and to keep it."[18] Thus even before the Fall, man had to work. For he had to "dress" Paradise. Therefore work was the duty of man from the first day of his life. It is not, then, the result of Original Sin; it is not a punishment for disobedience. On the contrary, work is closely related to the rational nature of man.

Since he was banished from Paradise, the life of man is also closely bound up with the duty of work. Man has to cultivate the soil from which he was taken. God renews His first declarations. Sin banished man from Paradise, but in doing so it did not exempt him from work.

To the ordinary duty of work is added difficulty in performance, unknown until then but which is the normal consequence of the corruption of the mind and the will through sin. There is a hint of God's sadness in this confirmation of the human lot: "By the sweat of thy brow shalt thou eat bread."[19]

Work is therefore an honorable summons by God to cooperation in the fulfilment of the divine plan. It is not a punishment, but is trust shown in man. It must not only preserve human life but satisfy all our needs.

[18] Gen. 2:15.

[19] Gen. 3:19.

Work as a Need of Human Nature

Man's rational nature calls him to work

Man comes into the world almost completely unprepared for life, incapable of preserving it, defenseless. The awakening of reason points out his potential in life. God put His trust in this mind, and thanks to it, man will have the ability to fend for himself on earth.

Reason will guide man in undertaking the work by which he has to earn the indispensable means for the maintenance and preservation of life. As a result of this, everything by which man is served is prepared by work for direct use.

It is enough to glance around us in order to notice everywhere the fruits of work. We see in them the whole appropriateness and usefulness of human effort. We see that work tends to give new values to things, that it adapts them to our needs. Appropriateness and usefulness are therefore the stimuli to work, just as they are the criteria of its worth. Thanks to this fact, work gives us a chance to satisfy hunger and thirst; it shelters us, raises a roof over our heads; it makes human life possible, easy, and pleasant.

But work has more than merely consumer aims. More than the mouth and the stomach compel man to work; our whole rational nature urges us to it. For work leads to the complete development of our spiritual powers and to the perfecting of man.

From time to time people are seized by a longing for those future happy times when work will show itself to be superfluous. Man's liberation from work is a tempting thought. People triumphantly emphasize the fact that work will be shorter and free time longer. They declare that human life should be arranged so that work will cease to be a phenomenon inseparable from it.

Is there not some misunderstanding here? There is inevitably a lowering of the value of work when it is respected not because of its lofty meaning for man but for the sake of the material profits to be derived from it. Christianity preaches a more complete understanding of work: if it exalts and elevates work, this is not merely because man finds in work the means of his own elevation, but also because work is the duty of the rational being, man, and because it is for him the way to reveal and develop all his spiritual gifts.

For work is strongly bound up with the human will. Actually there is no work in the strict meaning of the word that it would be possible to separate from man. Even the work of the most elaborate machine depends on the supervision and help of a rational being. The contemporary plans of technicians, which organize factory work in such a way that it needs the smallest number of people, are in fact achieving amazing results. But, in the end, even in the most technologically perfect factory, it is human vigilance, human thought, and human actions (insignificant perhaps at times, but irreplaceable nevertheless) that determine the worth of these elaborate automatons. So it remains true that almost every kind of work is bound up with a human being.

Our mind, will, feeling, and physical strength share in work. We have really got the ideal picture of the working man when none of these gifts is barred from participation in the course of work. The upsetting of this balance will always be detrimental to a man and even to his work itself.

Of course, the kind of work we do determines the degree of participation our mind, will, feeling, or physical powers have in it. But there is no work from which they can be fully separated.

Unfortunately, such attempts have sometimes been made. Under the influence of technological development in the organization of the workshop, man is being increasingly relegated to the role of an additional instrument, which comes last in importance. When following the so-called rules of the scientific organization of work, it is often forgotten that this is not the organization of some abstract force but is actually the organization of human work.

Man is being subjected to the laws of technology and mechanized in his acts and movements to such an extent that his work has almost lost its rational character.

Some even think that the mind of man is sometimes an impediment to the smooth running of work. Work has become so simplified, so thoughtlessly monotonous, that the mind has nothing to hold onto in it. In the factory, they say, man's mind is unnecessary; only his strength is needed. The acts performed are so mechanical that the human mind with its thoughts and interests rather interrupts the process: man, the rational being, is now superfluous. Technology, which is the new god, wins. Technology has gone from being the triumph of the human brain to being its enemy. Maybe this is because it has freed itself from the natural laws that bind it. Human work should be organized in such a way that the whole man can express himself in it. For this is the interior need of the rational being.

There must be a place for human thought in every kind of work. When we deprive ourselves of thought we impoverish both ourselves and society, in which, for this very reason, the number of people unaccustomed to using their mind in everyday affairs is increasing. The world is changing into a society of automatons. People are losing their sense of belonging to a community.

In all well-organized work there must also be room for a full understanding of it. The human mind and will should derive something from work. The command that has been received must be subjected to the judgment of the reason. For reason points out to us the best ways of doing our work; it shows us how to perfect its performance. So-called blind obedience in work, freeing man from the need to think for himself, only in very exceptional circumstances fails to be detrimental.

Likewise the use of physical strength has to be subjected to human reflection, for only under the influence of feeling and will is the use of strength rational and fitting. In other words, work has a human character only when all of our faculties are joined together in it.

Work perfects man and his acts

It is the working man himself who most benefits from work understood in this way. This is not because he gets his wages for his work, but because his work, which is bound inseparably with his person, shapes and develops his mind, will, feelings, and various moral virtues and characteristics, as well as his physical and spiritual skills. This is what St. Paul means when he reminds us that "the first share in the harvest goes to the laborer who has toiled for it."[20] We gather the first fruits ourselves.

The organizers of every kind of work should rely not only on our obedience but also on those particular virtues that, together with our reason and freedom, should develop in us under the influence of the work we do.

Work, based on our reason and freedom, should develop our conscientiousness, our sense of duty, and our responsibility. Only then will it be the work of a rational being.

Work, understood in this sense, immediately reveals to us two aims that every man ought to achieve in his personal work: the perfecting of things and the perfecting of the working man. This is the starting point for social-economic progress, for human civilization, for moral-religious progress, and indeed for the culture of the world.

In work we bring things to perfection and goods to completion. We wish to bestow a new usefulness, a new value and perfection on things. For only then does work achieve its aim, and herein lies

[20] 2 Tim. 2:6.

all its meaning. By conferring a new worth on matter, work becomes the sole author of wealth, well-being, and national abundance. All that exists around us has to acquire new values by the will of God: "Fill the earth, and subdue it."[21] Man's worth in fact is reflected in human acts. From economic progress, and from the direction this progress is taking, we can make out how a man is developing and what his worth is. Every man betrays himself in the value he gives to things.

But the perfection of matter and of things is not the only aim of human work. Its second aim is the perfecting of the person who is doing the work.

Work is one of the means of our spiritual progress. It has to be performed in such a way that man becomes better not only in the sense of physical efficiency but also in the moral sense.

This truth is almost completely forgotten today. The myth of payment for work has conquered all of us: payment by the hour, piecework, salaries, fees. Man is lost in the pursuit of profit, driven by "duty," which he often understands rather as a sense of external need than as a moral value. Moreover, we are becoming the slaves of things. We are so absorbed in and engrossed by the perfecting of what we do that we completely forget about ourselves. We even consider that excessive work frees us from the duty of molding our own souls.

As a result, man modifies nothing in himself. In *Quadragesimo Anno*, Pius XI drew attention to one of our many contemporary contradictions: the fact — in which the unhappiness of the world today consists — that while dead matter emerges from the economic workshop ennobled, man, on the other hand, is made worse, and becomes more vulgar.[22]

[21] Gen. 1:28.

[22] Pius XI, *Quadragesimo Anno*, section 153.

Working Your Way into Heaven

It is true that many wonderful works of human hands and of the human soul are to be seen around us. Yet the world works but does not change. In this way, it departs from God's plan. So it is not strange that man neither becomes happy nor feels well as a result of the work of his hands.

There is only one solution: to break with the notion that assigns only one aim to work (that is, the satisfaction of the needs of our existence), and to return to the one real judgment by which work is not so much a sad necessity and a mere safeguard against hunger and thirst, as it is a need of the rational nature of man, who gets to know himself fully through work, and learns to express himself completely in it. And it is only then that he can influence matter in a really fitting and useful manner.

The fruits of work that is thus understood will not be wasted or badly used but will become a blessing for the world.

4

Work as a Social Duty

The former picture would be incomplete if we did not come to see its other side. Man (a being consisting not only of a soul but of a body as well) is, from the very nature of his personality, a social being. Everything connected with human life must respond to this social character.

Work has a social dimension

In the same way, all human activity reflects in itself the dual character of man's personality. This activity is directed to his own ends and, at the same time, it goes beyond those aims by going out to his neighbor. Thus our work acquires not merely a personal but a social character as well.

Man tends with all his soul and body not only toward himself, but also toward creation, his neighbor, and God. This is particularly noticeable in the sphere of our daily work. There arises in our work, because of it and with its help, a distinct bond among people, the social bond.

What is this in reality? It is easier to observe and describe it than to define its nature. When we are working with others, there is some force that binds them together around us and unites us with them. The man without work, the idle man, is usually isolated. A man at work has people crowding around him, like bees around the queen. Work binds man to man: there is no doubt about this.

Work creates bonds between persons

There is no work in the performance of which man can be shut up wholly in himself. In every type of human work there is a bond with some other work that has already been done — a connecting link in the work itself: work done before this present work binds together the past and the future. No matter what we take up in the course of our work, we always see in it, enclosed in its completed form, the embodied work of the past. The work that we add to the work already done, will itself be taken up by our successors, who will develop it, improve it perhaps, and bring it one stage further. In the same way, a man at work now is linked with the man who worked before him and with the man who will work after him. There is a sort of special "communion of saints" in and through work. This is the historical bond.

But in every kind of work we notice more than just the bond of material achievements. Above all, the common bond of human thought is contained in work. In almost every work we try to find out its principal motives, the thought contained in it. But we also implant in it a new thought, our own, which we sow in it as the farmer sows grain in the soil. This thought perhaps will only become embodied in the future and will only yield a hundredfold to generations yet unborn. We accept the work of our predecessors with all respect and we try to discover their innermost thoughts, to get the feeling of the spirit of their actions. Just so did architects carry out faithfully the thought that was born in the hearts of their predecessors and enclosed in the harmonious and compact lines of Gothic cathedrals, which were sometimes finished or restored centuries after they were begun. It is just the same with every act of human hands and brains.

The bond of work is based on love

The bond that arises in human work is the radiance of love. For work itself is indeed love; it is the showing-forth, the witnessing of love. Love, hidden in work that is at times burdensome and boring, does not always betray its presence, for dust and sweat cover its brightness. Yet how often does it reveal itself, not only at the moment when some new work comes to birth, but even in the pain of completing old ones.

Work is man's tendency to draw near his fellowman; it cannot aim at emptiness. It always links us with people — if not immediately, then at least indirectly. There can be no work that in some mysterious way does not link us with people, even the work that is directed toward God. In fact, that kind of work especially links us with people.

Work is a social service

Work teaches us mutual service and provides us with a chance to perform it. Through associating with our neighbors we come to feel the need of service and the desire to serve others. We would be very ashamed and humiliated if we could not pay our debt by some type of work. Our mutual need and our usefulness are emphasized in the bond of work. We continually realize our helplessness and inadequacy. Have we not many needs whose satisfaction depends on those around us? There is nothing strange in the fact that in return for a glass of water given to our brother,[23] Jesus rewards us with the kingdom of Heaven: for this service contains the whole truth of our dependence and our insufficiency, the truth of the indispensable services we do to others or that others do to us. For the cup of favors received we repay with a cup of favors returned. And this binds and unites us to people. Work, which teaches us love, dependence, and humility, compels us to be of use to one another and so creates human society. In this society work acquires new possibilities of development through the adjustment, division, and intensification of combined human efforts. This then is the social bond, the brotherhood of people through work.

Work promotes the universal good

The social meaning of work is not only contained in the creative bond of work between men, but is also to be found in a special way in the fruits of work.

Work must create universal good. What does this mean? We understand by it the attainment of the goal that God set Himself when He created the world and human life on earth. God, as the creator and organizer of the world from the very beginning, has a plan toward which He is guiding the whole world. The realization of this plan of God's, in the natural as well as in the supernatural order, is the achievement of the final and universal good.

Related to this highest good there are also other goals that man decides to obtain for himself, namely, partial goods of which he wants to gain possession. These are the goods of the family, profession, nation, and state. Man attains these goods through cooperation with other men who are striving toward the same

[23] Matt. 10:42.

goal. To achieve various good things, man can combine his efforts in societies, meetings, associations, etc. All the goods achieved as a result of people's cooperation must be brought into conformity with God's plan.

It is actually human work that has to bring this agreement about, that has to aim at the good planned by the paternal Providence of God. In this sense our work will be service to God, to ourselves, and to our neighbor, within the limits determined by God's plan. It will be cooperation with God in the spirit of His command "Fill the earth, and subdue it."[24]

The summons to work on this earth is God's general mobilization. When God announced this summons He saw the earth as it would become through work. God saw races, generations, tribes, and nations, whole ages and epochs that would go through the world in submissive service to Him, adding ever more perfection, wrought by His power in work, to what He had made. God mobilized the thoughts and will of rational man — man who looks into the future and whose conquering toil extends not only over his own needs but over the needs of those who will inhabit the earth after him. By so doing God ensured that there would be provisions for the unborn generations, that the earth would really be subject to His fatherly care, that it would bring forth all that was necessary so that man, living on earth, could attain Heaven.

"Fill the earth and subdue it." That is to say, acquire the means that make life possible for you up to that unknown moment when, having left to the living the good things you have attained, you give yourselves up wholly to God.

"Fill the earth and subdue it." Create such conditions of life as allow you to achieve the perfection of this life, and with it, freedom to strive toward God.

[24] Gen. 1:28.

This endeavor sums up the most important temporal elements of the universal good — the satisfaction of physical needs so that man may, without hindrance, devote himself to the worship of God. In this highest of goods, which is eternal salvation, the needs of all men find their fulfilment.

Service through work widens our hearts and embraces all our neighbors in a spirit of love for their souls and bodies, their temporal and eternal good.

Man has a duty to be socially useful through work

Everyone is continually receiving help, both from those close at hand and from those far off. Man benefits by material goods as much as by the moral, cultural, and national legacy created by whole generations of people of whom he may never have heard. He lives by their work, their effort, their zeal, their devotion, and their sacrifice — even by the sacrifice of their lives.

There are no good things that should be foreign to a Christian. We draw on them continually; they make life possible for us. It would be selfishness to accept all this calmly, without any desire to show our gratitude. We must pay our debt by helping our neighbors through the fruits of our work. And this is how work is shared among men. Our work sets out to be useful, which means that it sets out to respond to our neighbors' need, to keep pace with the multitude of services that we have received from them.

Work provides the means to help our neighbors

The social character of our work is seen in the fact that it has to provide the means for helping our neighbors. This aim is what distinguishes the Christian philosophy of work and constitutes its whole splendor and breadth of outlook, its whole social spirit.

Naturally, the fruits of work are intended first of all to satisfy the personal needs of every man. This is not selfishness, but charity properly apportioned. Yet we are not entitled to the whole of these fruits. We share them with our family and with those close to us to whom we are bound by the duty of charity and justice. Within the boundaries of the family we include not only children and relations, but the entire household, everybody who works with us and helps us to achieve the fruits of our work.

Any further yield from our work must be shared especially with those who are incapable of work and who, through no fault of their own, cannot earn the necessities of life. And here again we see how much higher the Christian ideal is than the pagan. Pagan practice tells us to do away with those who are incapable of working. The Christian ideal, on the other hand, calls us to remember God's plan: "To thee is the poor man left: thou wilt be a helper to the orphan."[25]

Certainly, the duty of work is bound up most closely with the support of our family. "The man who makes no provision for those nearest him, above all his own family, has contradicted the teaching of the Faith, and indeed does worse than the unbelievers do."[26] These are strong words, showing how strong the bond is between us and those in our immediate neighborhood. At the same time they are the basis of social order and a secure existence, for they call forth all our ardor and energy in giving aid to others. Without delay, without hesitation, "let us practice generosity to all, while the opportunity is ours; and above all, to those who are of one family with us in the Faith."[27] These thoughts should inspire us in our work, and should be a stimulus to victory over weaknesses of

[25] Ps. 9:14 (RSV = Ps. 10:14).

[26] 1 Tim. 5:8.

[27] Gal. 6:10.

will, mind, and heart, and over any dislikes or prejudices that might arise; so that, with this inspiration, there should be no lack of the full measure of charity in the use that we make of the fruits of our work.

This regulates and purifies the intentions for which we work; it directs them, in God's name, toward all our neighbors. When Christian thought is the motivation for our work it makes us go beyond the narrow circle of our household. For work should give us the means to practice charity, and as the social encyclicals tell us, those who cannot work must avail themselves of the toil of those who can.

It is this thought that gives to human work its most sublime character. It cleanses our work of selfishness, of greed for profit, of the spirit of materialism and worldliness. Our work must be filled with the spirit of love, of sacrifice, of disinterestedness, of service to those who cannot work, of service to the poor, to orphans, and to those who are unfit for effort and toil, especially the sick. The poor are God's family. They are in His care. And He exercises His care over them through our hands, abilities, talents, zeal, industry, and love.

The depths of Christian love are here fully revealed. God has trusted me! "I give thee strength, abilities, and desires, so that through them thou mayst serve others." But there is also the duty to "work instead, and earn by your own labor the blessings you will be able to share with those who are in need."[28]

A new incentive to work! It is this that leads man out of the narrow backyard of his own purely personal affairs onto the broad highways of love. Through it, we become God's family in work. We know very well that the more efficient our work is, the more means Providence acquires to distribute to the poor and the needy.

[28] Cf. Eph. 4:28.

This is the starting point for Christian zeal in work, for Catholic effort, intensity, and heroism in work. "He who sows sparingly, will reap sparingly; he who sows freely will reap freely too. Each of you should carry out the purpose he has formed in his heart, not with any painful effort; it is the cheerful giver God loves. . . . He who puts grain into the sower's hand, and gives us food to eat, will supply you with seed and multiply it, and enrich the harvest of your charity."[29]

[29] 2 Cor. 9:6-7, 10.

5

The Use of the Fruits of Work

Work in its social character expresses itself in property, but property passes in turn through our hands to the advantage of our neighbor.

St. Paul outlined the process that unites people in work in these words from his letter to the Ephesians: "Let each man work instead, and earn by his own labor the blessings he will be able to share with those who are in need."[30]

The possession of some property binds one closely to God's ordering of the world; the conditions of human life are to a great extent bound up with some sort of possession.

It is not at all strange that the Church defends the law of private property, although on the other hand, it weakens the "proprietary" spirit as an excessive development that arises out of the application of the law of private property. Besides, what we are speaking of now is the common use of goods that are possessed individually.

[30] Eph. 4:28.

Work leads to possession

This whole problem is closely allied to the proper interpretation of work, for work usually leads to possession. The aim of possession is the satisfaction of our own needs and those of our family and the sharing of what is left over with our neighbors. Possession becomes ennobled through the duty of charity, and through this both man and his work are ennobled and cleansed from selfishness and the desire for personal profit.

For a full picture of the value of human work we must notice the Pauline motive in that work: to have the means to give to the needy. This lies at the basis of the Catholic concept of property, which is so different from that in capitalist thought.

Private property should serve the common good

Private possession and common usage of goods is the leading principle of a well-regulated society. For the preservation of order in society, God willed that man's right to possession should become divided in this manner. He expressed His will in the nature of things and in the nature of human needs. Private property is protected by the law of custom, by public arrangement, and by the law of God. Man can defend his right with the help of distributive justice. Thanks to this fact, external order and the just usage of the goods of this earth are protected.

However, although shielded by justice, the law of property is still burdened by social duty. For although human work and property are intended for the satisfaction of our own needs, a certain amount of goods generally remains unused. And no man is free to do just what he likes with these surplus goods. Everyone has a duty to use what is left over for social purposes, in the spirit of the love of one's neighbor, of charity, and of magnanimity.

To the extent that private property is guarded by the virtue of justice, the use of goods is governed by the virtue of love and the duty of almsgiving, charity, and magnanimity. Indeed, thanks to these virtues, which govern the use of our own goods, the usage of goods is common and is guided by social love.

Love should be the basis of work and property

This same spirit, which governs the use of property, must inform human work. We do not work merely to earn the necessities of life for ourselves, but the thought of our neighbors' need should also accompany us in our work. "Let each man work instead, and earn by his own labor the blessings he will be able to share with those who are in need." We gain thereby a new stimulus to work, thanks to which the goal of our work becomes more profound. Our neighbors have to live by the work of our hands. The fruits of our work also serve the people immediately around us. This is the special commandment of our time, to conquer the selfishness of the goals that many people pursue in their work, to master low greed, to ennoble effort and competition, to encourage conscientiousness, to raise the productivity of our work beyond the limit of our own, perhaps modest, needs. The teaching of the social encyclicals aims at spiritualizing the effort of human work, so that man at work does not shut himself up in himself.

The spirit of monastic poverty must include this same will to serve one's neighbors through work, and this today is the special task of the times. Monastic life must develop along lines that are suited to new social needs and that will help to fill them. Society has its poor and its beggars, who possess no means of existence. In keeping the vow of poverty we should be inspired by the will to serve our neighbors in the spirit of Paul's directive. We should do what we can to strengthen the will to compassion, cooperation, and solidarity with the poor. We should work eagerly and zealously so that we may be better able to help the needy. We should take on ourselves work, effort, and toil so that we have something to give to the poor.

This program is both old and new. It is bound up with what was once known and practiced, and was destroyed by the spirit of economic calculation. For even in pre-Christian times, under the influence of God's wisdom, these thoughts guided the efforts of human work.

Scripture exhorts us to almsgiving

The principle of the common usage of goods and of work for the benefit of our neighbors is not new, as many passages of Holy Scripture show. We are struck by two duties that we find there: almsgiving and work done that there may be something to give to the poor. First of all, there is the duty of almsgiving out of the goods that we possess.

Job, while examining his conscience, cannot find a cause for his sufferings in his neglect of the duty of almsgiving. "If I have denied to the poor what they desired, and have made the eyes of the widow wait, if I have eaten my morsel alone and the fatherless hath not eaten thereof (for from my infancy mercy grew up with me and it came out with me from my mother's womb), if I have despised him that was perishing for want of clothing and the poor man that had no covering, if his sides have not blessed me and if he were not warmed with the fleece of my sheep, . . . let my shoulder fall from its joint."[31]

Tobias the elder, when giving advice on life to his son, tells him clearly, "Eat thy bread with the hungry and the needy, and with

[31] Job 31:16-22.

thy garments cover the naked."[32] This is, as it were, preparing the way for Christ's counsel: "The man who has two coats must share with the man who has none; and the man who has food to eat, must do the like."[33]

The spirit of almsgiving is stressed on every page of Sacred Scripture and reaches its highest point in the description — so characteristically treated — of the Last Judgment, where material services, performed out of love for God, are finally seen at their true value.[34]

Of necessity, it follows that with private possession goes the duty of using goods in common through almsgiving. But more noteworthy still is the duty of work itself to multiply goods for our neighbors' needs, so that we have more to share with them.

The Mosaic Law plainly set out that the poor must eat from the work of our hands. "Six years thou shalt sow thy ground, and shalt gather the corn thereof. But the seventh year thou shalt let it alone, and suffer it to rest, that the poor of thy people may eat, and whatsoever shall be left, let the beasts of the field eat it."[35]

This regulation is peculiar, and offends our economic calculations. Man has a duty to work, but out of this work he has to share with his neighbors and even with animals. This also helps us to understand the spirit of common usage.

How subtle and farseeing a love of one's neighbor is contained in the Old Testament commandment, which may displease many present-day agronomists: "When thou reapest the corn of thy land, thou shalt not cut down all that is on the face of the earth to the very ground; nor shalt thou gather the ears that remain.

[32] Tob. 4:17.

[33] Luke 3:11.

[34] Matt. 25: 35-46.

[35] Exod. 23:10-11.

Neither shalt thou gather the branches and grapes that fall down in thy vineyard, but shalt leave them for the poor and the strangers to take. I am the Lord your God."[36]

In the book of Ruth we read that Boaz deliberately ordered his harvesters to leave corn in the fields, so that Ruth, who was poor, would have some to bring home.[37] This picture illustrates the interesting practice that obtained in those days.

Or we might consider the right that passersby had to take ears of corn or grapes from others' fields: "Going into thy neighbors' vineyard, thou mayst eat as many grapes as thou pleasest, but must carry none out with thee. If thou go into thy friend's corn, thou mayst break the ears, and rub them in thy hand, but not reap them with a sickle."[38] Here once again is a strikingly social custom, which was preserved down to the time of Christ and of which He Himself made use.[39]

We should live frugally to share more with the poor

How very far we have moved today from this sympathy with the poor! Certainly, economic progress brings with it new ideas, but what concerns us here is not the preservation of old customs, but rather of their spirit. And this spirit is singularly social, favorable to the poor and to human needs, to "passersby, widows, and orphans."[40] Property is preserved and respected; the soil and its fruits belong to the owner. But he must work with his neighbor in mind; he must share what he has, gladly. Our work should be

[36] Lev. 19:9-10.

[37] Ruth 2.

[38] Deut. 23:24-25.

[39] Mark 2:23.

[40] Deut. 24:19-21.

transformed by the thought that we must make it more productive, so that we may be better equipped to help our neighbors. Even when the burden of excessive work weighs on us, the memory of our needy brothers raises our spirits and brings relief.

There is one more immensely important consideration that gives rise to the virtue of generosity. Pius XI in his encyclical *Quadragesimo Anno* tells us that if, when our own needs have been satisfied according to our station in life, there are still goods left over (savings, capital, and similar commodities), we do not have complete freedom to do what we like with them; we have a duty to employ them to create new possibilities of work for our neighbor.[41] The Christian spirit requires us to curb our selfishness in the possession and use of goods; it demands broader thinking and greater sensitivity to the needs of society.

An illustration of this principle is the example of the Gospel householder who sent the unemployed to his vineyard, although there was no real need for them there. He was guided not so much by the spirit of strict need or justice, as by a spirit of magnanimity and generosity. One reservation the Pope makes is that capital should be assigned to the production of really useful goods.[42]

In the encyclical *Divini Redemptoris*, Pius XI reminds us of the duty of limiting one's own needs, of returning to more frugal conditions of life, so as only to acquire the means of giving social help.[43] To forget oneself for love of one's neighbor, to limit luxury, so shocking side-by-side with poverty: this is the new task. Our life should be simplified, set free from the superfluity of things and artificial needs that are swamping us. Life must triumph over the state of its impoverished surroundings.

[41] Pius XI, *Quadragesimo Anno*, section 53-54.

[42] Ibid., section 54.

[43] Pius XI, *Divini Redemptoris*, section 90.

6

Human Work as Cooperation with God

We are at the turning point of our considerations. Paul's words will serve us as a signpost: "Stand firm, then, my beloved brethren, immovable in your resolve, doing your full share continually in the task that the Lord has given you, since you know that your labor in the Lord's service cannot be spent in vain."[44]

Let us look at work now from God's point of view — God who is a witness of our work, and in whose presence it is carried out.

All this so-called work of ours is not actually our work at all. For we can only call "ours" what belongs to us fully and unconditionally, what depends on us and is directed toward us.

Now our work does not belong to us wholly. For even in the most personal work we use powers and strength that are given to us by God, the Creator of nature. This work does not belong to us, for its character is not only personal but social as well. Neither can we wholly divert our work toward ourselves. So when we speak of "our work" we are allowing ourselves some exaggeration. It is

[44] 1 Cor. 15:58.

rather a simplification of our thought than a literal expression of the truth.

The toil of human work is cooperation with God

The following words recall this fact: "Work at all your tasks with a will, reminding yourselves that you are doing it for the Lord, not for men; and you may be sure that the Lord will give the portion He has allotted you in return."[45]

God is the cause of all creation and the giver of strength and energy for work. He also directs human energies toward the plans He had established in the act of creation. God has called us to cooperate with Him, and granted us appropriate powers, abilities, and the initial preparation for work. He still governs the world that He has created, and carries out part of His government with the help of man.

The Creator guides the world toward the goal that He has assigned to it. Only He knows the world fully and has its complete image in His mind. He sees its final perfection. For the achievement of this perfection the Creator guides the activities of the masses in their millions, whom He animates with the will of cooperation.

Around us we see the immensity of creation and the immensity of the work that has been done. In the face of all the work performed in the world we feel like a man who unexpectedly finds himself in a factory full of machinery. He becomes dazed, seeing all the dizzy movement and impetus of transmission belts transferring energy, and hearing all the noise and the whirring. It makes him uneasy; he feels helpless and powerless. He has to be led into the mystery and purposefulness of all this effort.

[45] Col. 3:23-24.

The created world is God's workshop

God's world works in peace and quietness. But when one really penetrates this work one feels continuous movement, the transmission of energy and of the powers of nature. We admire the greatness of the forces at work, their splendor, their arrangement and interrelation, their planning and order. We stand astonished at the threshold of God's workshop. We need someone to take us by the hand and explain the process and intention of all this commotion.

We look at God's work in too profane a manner. We take in the external phenomena of work and do not perceive the thought or guiding hand behind it. And all the while "the spirit of the Lord hath filled the whole world."[46]

The world is filled with the voice of God. Everything lives by God's activity. God's thought and intention can be recognized here. A moment's close examination reveals this thought to us, this great diversity and wonder of God's activity in the world. These are not "blind forces," as we are accustomed to say. They are all controlled by God and brought toward Him in a full and complete manner.

In the act of creation we see the divine thoroughness. There is nothing shoddy or intermittent here. Everywhere there is an abundance of the real perfection that things should have: "God's works are perfect."[47] God has displayed this perfection before our eyes as if He wanted to say, "Go and see how I work."

The created world is a living example, lesson, and education for us. The very sight of its creatures has an educational effect, for we admire in them the complete perfection of God's activity.

[46] Wisd. of Sol. 1:7.

[47] Cf. Rev. 15:3.

God does not merely aim at purely useful work but is mindful of beauty and decoration — there is aestheticism in what He does. Everything brings home to us the beauty with which God ornaments the works He has created. It is not only the heavens that tell of God's glory.[48] We see it in the tiniest creature here on earth. This beauty has to hold our attention; it has to compel us to meditation.

But it does not end there. Man is called to more than mere admiration of God. God has called us to cooperation. "Away with you to the vineyard like the rest."[49] The world and everything that happens in it is God's vineyard. We must take a share in the Creator's work.

Our work helps complete God's work

Man is in God's service. When God says to us, "Fill the earth, and subdue it,"[50] He is, in this way, binding us to the earth and at the same time obliging us to work and cooperate with Him, so that the earth will really be subject to man, and through man, to God.

Man has to act according to God's plan; he has to perform what God has in mind for him. It is important therefore to remember in work that we are in God's service. It is important for us to know God's plan.

Human work is, moreover, a further stage of God's creative work; it is the process that completes the act of creation. God conceived the world in such a way that He gave us in enormous measure the power of taking the act of creation one stage further toward that degree of perfection that He had in mind. Although

48 Ps. 18:2 (RSV = Ps. 19:2).

49 Matt. 20:4.

50 Gen. 1:28.

God's own acts are perfect in themselves, it is necessary, if they are to be used rightly, to prepare them for their own proper use. And here there is room for man to share in the further shaping of God's activity.

The world is perfect in itself, but without the work of man it would not achieve its aim. It would not attain the measure of perfection proper to itself; instead, it would change into a jungle or a wild desert.

The earth calls for human work

The earth requires human work to reveal its real face. Our poor emigrants were spreading civilization when they cleared away the immemorial forests of the New World. These are the forms taken by the nonstop progress of the man of action. Thanks to the will to work, man is always seeking new territories for his activities. Admittedly, some say that the world is being choked by too many people, but God alone knows how far from completion the plan for the conquest of the whole earth still is. And it is God alone who knows all the possibilities of the earth; He sees it "all clothed in readiness, like a bride who has adorned herself to meet her husband."[51] And therefore God still maintains the law of life in man, the will to pass life on, knowing well that the wanderings of nations will conquer more and more stretches of land, will bring them into civilization, continually fulfilling the command "Fill the earth, and subdue it" — the whole earth, with all its seas, mountains, and deserts. Those countries that are wild today are certainly the sites for future states and rich cities. Who knows whether there may not flourish there, in the future, some wonderful civilization of whose form we have no inkling today? These are

[51] Rev. 21:2.

matters known only to the King of Ages! For God, all of our modern culture, which dazzles and makes us dizzy, may be merely childish prattle, the primer from which future ages will take a few letters for the creation of a new language of history. Perhaps some day they will say of us what we say of prehistory: "Those people of the twentieth century — they were real barbarians!"

The world in God's thought must undergo a further transformation with the help of human work carried out in the name of this same command, "Fill the earth, and subdue it." It seems to us that this is the commandment that people keep most faithfully. Even if they have rejected all the other commandments, in their work of conquering the earth they will always acknowledge the eternal sovereignty of God over the world and display obedience to the will of God.

Man must prepare the earth for human life and for God

Man must humanize the earth to prepare it, so that it is really worthy of its Creator and suitable for human life. Only when the face of the earth is stamped with the imprint of man's work does it become worthy of God, for it is man alone who is called to restore the earth to God.

The Creator gets back the glory due to Him from the earth, when it is civilized and filled with good and faithful servants — His children.

The Creator wants the world to be populated and filled abundantly: "Increase and multiply and fill the earth."[52] There will be more workers for the earth then, and more worshippers for God. The more work is done on the earth, the more possibilities of life there are on it, the more room for new people, the more means and

[52] Gen. 1:28.

goods to support life. And thus the world will be filled with peoples and nations.

Work makes possible our abundant population

And for what? Oh, we are insatiable! For we would be glad to see every day more sons of God praising their Creator, thanking Him for their daily bread, for their divine sonship, for the kingdom of Heaven, for immortality, for "life everlasting," which is to be filled with happiness without limit. We want this! We demand great numbers of people, because every human life means one more eternal happiness, one more man knowing real joy, one more infinite love of God.

We not only want people for the earth, in order to show the whole beauty and power of God's creation through their work, but we want people for Heaven also. And there is so much room in Heaven! Whoever has an open heart, and loves God without reserve, is not afraid of new people, of children, cribs, or the abundant population of the earth. He wants as many people as possible so that Heaven may one day possess its "millions of millions."

Here we are already thinking of the future glory of God. We think of this joy that is in waiting. We want God's plan to be completed here below.

And therefore abundant population does not terrify us, for every person is a son of God and His worshipper. If one has faith in God's Providence and in the wisdom of creation, one is confident that God is preparing a splendid place for every one of those sons and that there will never be any shortage of bread. This will encourage in us the will to work, and will stimulate effort and thought, so that we can cooperate with the Father of creation in the task of feeding the human race. The Catholic will in life is the will to work; it is the source of progress in the world, and of the further development of civilization and culture.

By cooperating with God, man adds, through his work, new values and possibilities to creation. The population of almost twelve million people that lived in pre-partition Poland did not have any better conditions of life than we have today, when, within far more limited boundaries, there are twenty-eight million. How many new and valuable properties have we found in our soil in the course of the last few centuries, how many proofs of God's generosity and goodness! We are continually taking new riches out of the earth, and discovering possibilities of even further development.

By adding new values to created things, we try to earn God's praise for ourselves "as a workman who does not need to be ashamed of his work."[53] We fulfil this task by grasping God's intention fully and recognizing His goals. In every work we must, with the help of our rational nature, sense what God intends in His work of creation, so that we may harmonize the rhythm of our work with God's.

And God intends "to give them their food at the appointed time."[54] He intends, with the aid of human hands, to fill the earth with good things; He intends to demonstrate His love for the world in an even higher and more perfect degree; He intends to unite us all in brotherly love, and to make us combine in work and comradeship; He intends to achieve the fullness of His glory through our work, and to bestow on us the fullness of eternal happiness.

When we grasp God's intentions and cooperate with Him, the heaviest work loses some of its burden; our face, beaded with

[53] 2 Tim. 2:15.

[54] Ps. 144:15 (RSV = Ps. 145:15).

sweat, lights up in a smile: "As the eyes of the handmaid are on the hands of her mistress, so are our eyes unto the Lord our God."[55]

Work takes on nobility, sublimity, and dignity. Even the dirtiest work becomes the service of God. God did not lessen His glory when He bowed down to the dust of the earth and took Adam from it. The lowest work bears the marks of humanity and of the sonship of God.

There is no intelligent, purposeful, and useful work that does not have this aspect of nobility. Wherever man is working — whether it be in the mine, on the land, in the kitchen, or in the factory — he is in contact with God's gifts; everywhere he perceives some radiance of God's love.

Work, understood in this way, brings us back with new faith to God, and justifies us by deeds. We understand that man is usually justified by deeds done in the light of faith. For here we do our "full share continually in the task the Lord has given us. . . . Labor in the Lord's service cannot be spent in vain."[56]

[55] Ps. 122:2 (RSV = Ps. 123:2).

[56] 1 Cor. 15:58.

7

Work as Love for the Creator

We turn our attention now to the spiritual life in work. In God's plan, work is one of the means of interior sanctification.

Sometimes work turns man from God

The value of work is generally judged from the material point of view, according to the amount and cash value of what it produces. The benefits it yields to the human person are, on the other hand, ignored, as if the whole value of work were something that did not affect man himself. Herein lies an impoverishment of the concept of work, and a one-sidedness of the view of work. If we lose our sensitivity to the values that work gives rise to in the person, how are we to assess the part that work plays in the interior life of man? In this field, work is often considered an obstacle to the interior life, for work dissipates it, and diverts it from God. Man, when he is forced into excessively heavy work, is, as it were, handicapped, wronged by God, for he cannot discover God in his work. In fact, the contemporary organization of work very often distracts man completely from God owing to its one-sided exploitation of the former's efforts and time.

It is true that man is not destined for prayer alone, but neither is he created for work alone. Man is made for both prayer and work. Work can be allied to sanctification, for the inner harmony of human life has a salutary influence on work.

Exterior work not only should not become an obstacle to man; on the contrary, it should help him to sanctification. The very fact that work takes up the larger portion of our life induces the thought that God could not arrange life in such a way that man has his back turned on Him for so long. The truth is to be found halfway between both extremes. So the problem arises of how to arrange our work in such a way that it serves our interior life and, indeed, becomes one of the means of our sanctification.

St. John's words are worthy of note: "The wages paid to him who reaps this harvest, the crop he gathers in, is eternal life, in which sower and reaper are to rejoice together."[57]

This seems strange at first. Of course, whoever reaps receives his wages; this is clear. But that he should gather the fruit unto life everlasting!

It is plain that everything we do has some connection with the sanctification of the human soul and profits us not only materially but spiritually. That, in fact, is how it is.

Work expresses our love for the Creator of all things

Work is the development and formation of love in oneself, and a wonderful opportunity of expressing to God our love for Him. For in work man becomes God's "wise and faithful servant,"[58] on

[57] John 4:36.
[58] Matt. 24:45.

the model of the Gospel servant whom his master entrusted with care of the household to ensure that it received its measure of wheat at the appointed time.

Every man who is performing useful and purposeful work is appointed to it by God, who calls us by a vocation or an inclination, a fancy or a sense of mission, or through compliance and obedience to our superiors. Man is appointed by different methods, so that his labor may bear some fruit.

From this it follows that everything that man does — provided that it is intelligent, noble, fitting, and useful — is embraced by the will of God. God has assigned to us a certain section of work, determined by duty, vocation, obedience, or inclination, that we might go and bring back fruit. The heavenly "Householder" settles accounts wonderfully with the workers under Him: "Since thou hast been faithful over little things, I have great things to commit to thy charge."[59] God entrusts us with the small details of temporal life and repays our faithfulness with life everlasting.

Therefore whatever we do, we should regard as being done on God's orders. Seeing things in this light, we must be faithful even in small matters; the great God ordained them and by faithfulness to God and love for Him, everything becomes great. For these little things are bound up in the plan and order of the world; they are included in God's thought and commands. God foresaw these things, gave the energy for them, allotted them a time and a place, and appointed their goal and executor. Man, by his submission, is the executor of God's universal plan in its details.

The greatness of our life in furthering God's plans does not depend on what we do, on what form our activity takes, but on how we perform our tasks. Tiny and insignificant achievements can make us great, while great ones, if they are badly performed,

[59] Matt. 25:23.

can degrade us. Those who are "faithful in little things" are also entitled to the reward of eternal happiness — which is the greatest reward there is.

From such trifles of life, when they are performed with a great heart, arises the greatness of man. This is a truth of no little weight in daily life, for in its name are undertaken the dull, dirty, wearisome jobs of the world, without which human life would become impossible. It gives patience, submissiveness, and humility to all those unknown workers whom the proud world values so little, but who are rightly convinced that no honest work can harm a man, for we are all capable of, and are all called to, higher things.

The value of a human act does not depend on what sort of work one does, but on how one does it, on the degree of one's love and submission to God.

Man, by his work, becomes God's friend

"And you, if you do all that I command you, are my friends."[60] Man wins God's friendship by every task that he does in submission to God, in concert with God's plan.

"I do not speak of you any more as my servants; a servant is one who does not understand what his master is about, whereas I have revealed to you all that my Father has told me; and I have called you my friends."[61] This can be seen particularly in work, by which we enter into a direct relationship with everything around us. We recognize the Creator in creation, in the ordering of the world's affairs in accordance with God's thought. We are obligated to carry out God's plans. This work is necessary to God; God intended it, that the world might fully respond to His temporal and eternal

[60] John 15:14.

[61] John 15:15.

purpose. The fulfilment of God's plan in the world is the revelation of friendship with God. And this is just what happens in every kind of human work that brings people closer and binds them together with the ties of fellowship and friendship.

We come to know God through our work

For labor brings one closer to creation, which is God's work. The book of Wisdom teaches us this: "For by the greatness of the beauty, and of the creature, the Creator of them may be seen, so as to be known thereby."[62]

In external work the link with the Creator's works becomes so close that this very link opens our eyes to the moving force behind the marvels of the world. Next to interior life, an active life is one of the most direct ways of bringing one close to God. God wished to make creation witness to His existence, like a voice saying to men, "There is a God." Even if there were no divine Revelation and teaching Church, creation would bear witness to the Creator. The closer people are to nature, the more strongly they sense the nearness of God.

People in the country are more religious not because they are less exposed to corruption, but because they are in closer touch with nature. We feel our full dependence on God when we work on a farm; we recognize more easily the richness and greatness of creation and its inner beauty. Those who have lost God will find Him again in the voices of nature. Let us read the poetry of Kasprowicz, Bak, and Staff, which is full of the testimony that nature bears to its Creator. It is fortunate that towns no longer impress people so much, and that men are returning to the "bosom of nature."

[62] Wisd. of Sol. 13:5.

We feel God in the various gifts we use in the effort of work. We adore God in the gift of physical strength, recognizing our dependence on the Creator in the most elementary conditions of our work: "Without me you can do nothing."[63] We feel God in the gifts of mind and will, which give us the ability to act and to arrive at an understanding of the created world and of those around us.

Our love for God is born from a deep knowledge of Him. Those whose lives are closely bound up with work usually have a greater love for God than have the idle. For in work we have the most vital contact with the goodness of God and with His love, which purifies and elevates us. From love is born the will for cooperation with God, for love consists in our surrendering our thought and will to Him. We approach God in our work, knowing that we can do all things, but only by relying on the help of God.

Work is an expression of our love of God

Work, undertaken from love of God and carried out in that spirit, is the high point of an active working life. It is a participation in the act of creation and in the work of God's Providence, that inconceivable work through which God by an act of His love keeps everything in existence.

With human work God brings His act of creation a step further. Man, in fact, creates nothing, for he is not omnipotent; but by his toil he causes the works that have been created by God to attain the perfection that is proper to them and to which they have been ordained. The cooperation of men with God's works enhances their effectiveness, because man "comprehending by the power of his reason things innumerable . . . governs himself by the foresight of his counsel, under the eternal law and the power of God, whose

[63] John 15:5.

Providence governs all things."[64] Man's cooperation helps to bring about the achievement of God's purpose. God willed that a rational being should go in among all the riches of nature and order them according to his own needs. God has need of human hands and legs, that with their help creation may reach the perfection that is His aim. In our work we usually forget about this loving cooperation with God; we do not realize that we are performing an act of love toward Him, that to some extent we are supplementing what I will be bold enough to call the "insufficiency" of God. And merely a little control will direct, in the fullest way possible, all our spiritual and physical powers to cooperation with God.

Work contributes to our salvation

Work, done for the love of God, is the participation of man not only in the act of creation, but also in the act of our salvation. For in every type of work, we experience toil and hardship that we can offer to God as a measure of atonement for human sins. The hardship of work flows from the clouding over of will and reason by Original Sin, and their consequent opposition to the laws of blessed work.

Should we want complete emancipation from this salutary hardship? Should we not realize rather that this work is due to God, as is our gratitude that the duty of work should be combined with the opportunity of restoring the order that was disrupted by sin? To accept the small amount of toil that is unavoidable even with the best organization of work, is to cooperate in the purification of our reason, will, and feelings, and to repair in ourselves whatever can be repaired in the course of work.

64 Leo XIII, *Rerum Novarum*. English translation in *Four Great Encyclicals* (New York: Paulist Press, 1931), 4.

Finally, it should be remembered that only the work that is undertaken out of love for God is salutary and meritorious. All other work, no matter how heroic, will not bring about man's salvation.

Our salvation will not be brought about even by heroic work undertaken with the future of the state in mind; it will not be brought about by painful, competitive toil, driven by the desire for profit or wages. It is regrettable that so great an effort, undertaken by millions of people, should neither cleanse them from guilt, nor free them from sin, nor atone to God, nor redeem, nor increase God's glory.

Work done without love has no power to redeem man from guilt. "In eating, in drinking, in all that you do, do everything for God's glory."[65] The smallest act can be sanctified by the intention that inspires it; it can bring merit with it and redemption, if its motive is the love of God. And on the other hand, spiritual, interior work, and even prayer itself, becomes materialistic and pagan when it is without love. Such are the mysteries of love, which lead us toward God through temporal affairs.

If the world were arranged otherwise it would long ago have become totally material and been lost. The value of human acts comes from the intention behind them. The lowest work can, through love, raise one to the heights of holiness, while the loftiest work, when it is performed without love, lowers and damns one. "I may give myself up to be burned at the stake; if I lack charity, it goes for nothing."[66]

Since our life is bound up with the immensity of daily work, since work is our blessing in the mind of God and a need of rational human nature, since work can raise man to the very peaks

[65] 1 Cor. 10:31.

[66] 1 Cor. 13:3.

of holiness, let the purest love for God guide it. Love shall be its beginning and fulfilment. For this, "every man shall receive a reward, and reap a harvest in everlasting life."[67]

[67] John 4:36.

8

Prayer through Work

There is no admonition that we meet with so often in the spiritual life as the words "Pray and work!" How many times have we been told to unite our work with prayer, to raise it up and sanctify it by prayer? Such frequent reminders flow from the real need and difficulty of safeguarding our interior life in the rush of work; we are frightened by this invasion, by the overwhelming nature of the work that is keeping us away from God. We long to preserve our spiritual life by permeating our work with prayer.

This thought is expressed in the maxim "Pray and work!" But this is a difficult thing to accomplish. For conscientiousness in work and the turning of our attention to God are at odds with one another. When we are fully absorbed in our work, we forget about everything, about the whole external world, and all the more about prayer.

Prayer in work, however, is not a kind of small change; it is not a half measure in the solution of this conflict, nor is it merely a supplement to work. Is it not a part of asceticism? Is it not true that prayer in work has a prominent place in the rules of contemplative orders and, at the present time, in the constitution of almost every religious society?

Prayer and work often conflict in modern life

This problem is especially timely. For the amount of external work is continually increasing. Our environment makes increasing demands on our services, human needs grow, and the love of one's neighbor, which, despite the evil in the world, is visibly spreading, draws us toward other people and encourages us to help them in their troubles.

As a result, the scale of both work and service is steadily increasing. In the life of our monasteries, the amount of time devoted to prayer in choir is being cut down all the time. And here the conflict arises: prayer or the service of one's neighbors? Hard-working nuns are in favor: they do "useful social work." Common prayer is being increasingly relegated to the sphere of private prayer; it is becoming a personal duty, although, fortunately, it is not growing less. But it is also getting harder to reconcile our other numerous duties with that of prayer, for which there is ever less room in the order of the day.

Although we all long for this "better part,"[68] we must yet concern ourselves with, and work at, many different things, as if we always had before us the image of the Last Judgment, when we shall be told, "when you did it to one of the least of my brethren, you did it to me."[69]

We insure ourselves against the future judgment of God, but also against the judgment of the world: we feed the hungry, give drink to the thirsty, clothe the naked, and accept the homeless

68 Luke 10:42.

69 Matt. 25:40.

into our own homes. But how does one reconcile social duties with one's interior life?

Prayer continues to be the greatest need of our soul, the most wonderful agent of sanctification, and the best way of adoring God. It must therefore continue to occupy its proper place; we cannot lose any part of it, in spite of the increasing deluge of work. We must, then, transfer it to the field of our work; it must "come out of the chapel," and go with us to our daily occupations.

And this is necessary for another reason: because our life is becoming increasingly disintegrated, because we are caught up in the condition of our work, which is full of effort and haste, and because we are surrounded by the bustle of the street, the courtyard, the school corridor, the boarding school, the hostel, and the soup kitchen. All that the day brings us has to be balanced by prayer, so that all this confusion will not be transferred to our souls and so that we may sanctify our work by prayer, and specifically by prayer in our work.

That is the problem! To solve it, let us recall those points of departure that we have already established for our problem.

The first is that our work is cooperation with God. Every activity brings us directly back to God's activity. And this is what is common both to work and to prayer, in which we also meet God.

Furthermore, to work is to enter into God's work, into the work of His creation. We are led into the center of God's life. And this does not take us out of the environment that surrounded us at prayer, for there also we entered into God's work, although it was of a different kind.

Still, work is recognition of God in His works. By recognition, love multiplies in us and that is why work is love. Do not the two meet in prayer?

Work and prayer are not alien to one another, therefore, even at the outset. In fact, prayer in work will only be a conclusion drawn from these truths; it will be both the necessity of work and at the same time its joy.

The love of God in our work has four consequences

If work leads to the love of God and one's neighbors, there are certain obvious consequences.

The first consequence is that if we love God in work, it is impossible not to tell Him so. It is hard to practice love in the silence of one's heart and thoughts. We cannot keep it a secret from God. Love must have its great avowal. And what is such an avowal but prayer?

From this prayer the soul rises up in song: "All ye works of the Lord, bless the Lord"[70] — all the works, and therefore, those also that are born of the work of human hands and brains.

The second consequence is that if we love God, we long to please Him by yielding to His will. And this is also inevitable. Besides, it is impossible to love by word and tongue. We love by deed and truth. We give evidence of our love in that we try to please God by our submission. For in work there is also great humility, compliance, and love. In the heavy toil of work we say to God, "This is how God is loved!"

The third consequence is that if we love God, interiorly we want to submit our life to Him completely. We want to do what He has in mind, to seek what He seeks, to perform what He wants, to feel oneself part of His plan and intention, to subordinate fully one's thoughts, feelings, strength, and human will to the commands of His will, and to act as He wishes! This, indeed, forms us inwardly in the image of God's activity to the fullest extent possible.

[70] Ps. 144:10 (RSV = Ps. 145:10).

Finally, the fourth consequence is that if we love God, we wish to have the same intention in our work as He has. To God's summons to "subdue the earth,"[71] we reply, "Not mine, but Thy will be done."[72] This intention of our work becomes its moral core. It gives to it its supernatural value. By our intentions, we sanctify our ordinary, everyday activities. "Whatsoever you do, do it from the heart, as to the Lord, and not to men."[73]

Prayer in work is a necessity

Prayer is a necessity of work, because work is love for people as well as for God. But there cannot be love for God without prayer. From this it follows that every loving work is prayer. The lack of prayer during work is a mistake that can be made in any activity.

The greater the love we have for God the more spontaneous prayer in work becomes. It is not necessary to look for it, to be encouraged to practice it, or to be reminded of it. As love increases in us, so the relation between every external action and the interior life is also increased. To some extent the consciousness of external action fades away and only the consciousness of prayer through work remains. So, in fact, to raise the level of love in work means to raise the level of prayer. For love completely envelops everything about us, and embraces our whole life, including all our actions and activities. Nothing escapes its embraces, for through love we become one with God, and, through prayer, everything that is "ours" becomes God's. "For all are yours. . . . and you are Christ's, and Christ is God's."[74]

[71] Gen. 1:28.

[72] Luke 22:42.

[73] Col. 3:23.

[74] 1 Cor. 3:22-23.

The necessity of prayer in work is linked with the consciousness of our insufficiency, with the toil and hardship of work. Without God we can do nothing — nothing either in the spiritual life or in the sphere of simple activity. God is the prime mover of every intention and act. From this comes our humility. We also know that "all our ability comes from God."[75] We also know that "nothing is beyond my powers thanks to the strength that God gives me."[76]

Faced by difficult tasks, when strength, merits, virtues, skill, and will are lacking, we are conscious of our resistance, grief, fatigue, and the deluge of work. The acceptance of this burden and the offering of it to God imposes itself on us like a joyful necessity. And again prayer becomes the intermediary. Simple working people have a habit of beginning every task, which will be more than ordinarily difficult, with a prayer. The farmer still kneels today on the ridge before he begins sowing; he makes the Sign of the Cross with the scythe before he begins to mow. The universal custom of the consecration of our fields of activity and our home is a distant echo of the living faith in the help of God.

For all those spiritual powers of ours that play a part in work are set in order by prayer. The mind embraces God's light. We know this fact well from more than mental work; the will, which is so perverse as a result of Original Sin, recovers its tendency toward what is good. Prayer exercises a special influence over our emotions and feelings, for our uncontrolled passions are revealed in work. We recognize our faults in it: slowness, laziness, love of comfort, impatience, lack of endurance, fickleness, and so on. When these faults are subjected to the cleansing power of prayer, peace returns; we brace ourselves with Christian courage for the

[75] Cf. Rom. 13:1.

[76] Phil. 4:13.

conquest of all opposition and hardship. It is not possible to do lasting, versatile, fruitful, and effective work without linking it with prayer.

Prayer in work brings joy

This is no small thing, for work-prayer is gratitude for the honor of our being called to cooperation with God; it is thanks for strength, health, the light of reason, wisdom, and the virtues and merits of the spirit that are drawn by our will into work.

Only when we use these things in our work as a musician uses the strings of his instrument, do we realize how great these gifts of God are. In work we see their usefulness; in work we recognize the value of the previous effort by which we acquired everything that we use today. Here the difference between virtue and imperfection can best be seen, between wisdom and knowledge on the one hand and ignorance on the other, between a strong and good will and the lack of will.

A man endowed generously by God, a man who has put much fruitful effort into his life, who has prepared himself for work by appropriate improvement and education, now reaps the fruits of his toil and devotion. And if, through his whole previous life, he responded readily to God's great graces, he enjoys the pleasures and results of his work all the more.

When, in addition, we see around us people who are unable to work — people who are longing to give themselves up to work, but whose strength does not allow it — the feeling of gratitude for the possibility of and vocation to work increases in us.

And thus a new good arises from our work: we see its worth, its usefulness. We see that the one Creator of all good is God. But we also see that, by the will of God, there is in almost every good a particle of recreative human work. Every good makes us rejoice.

Every achievement, every fruit of work, brings with it a natural reward in the form of tremendous joy. The first feeling is gratitude to God, the turning of every fruit of work to the glory of God. "To the one God praise and glory."[77] "All ye works of the Lord, bless the Lord."[78]

Work is a sacrificial surrendering to God at His bidding and direction. We know from experience that there is always joy linked with this readiness and sacrifice, particularly when, in the middle of a host of commitments, additional work falls on us — proof, as it were, of the trust of others and of God in us. To accept this in all readiness, to guide it toward the heavenly Father, is to express oneself with one's whole soul, a soul that is full of trust and loving prayer: "The Lord is my helper."[79]

The raising up of the thought, will, and heart to God in heavy daily work — this is the most noble form of adoring God.

All these thoughts go to create a whole system of the asceticism of work. Considered separately, they may seem to be something disconnected and artificial. They acquire their peculiar color and form, however, only when they are known through one's own experience. There will always be as many rich possibilities in the world as there are people and different kinds of work, as there are different stages of love and surrender to God.

Every man can create, against the background of his own life, his own world of prayer in work; every one solves this problem in a different way. For an understanding of prayer in work can be arrived at more by a life of work than by wordy discussions.

Indeed, it is not words, but only work itself, based on the love of God, that instructs us as to how we ought to pray in work. Then

[77] Cf. Ps. 95:7 (RSV = Ps. 96:7).

[78] Ps. 144:10 (RSV = Ps. 145:10).

[79] Ps. 117:6 (RSV = Ps. 118:7); Heb. 13:6.

the bidding "Pray and work" will cease to be simply a solemn command; then prayer will no longer be merely a supplement to work. Prayer transforms our work inwardly, and sanctifies it; and work widens the frontiers of prayer.

9

The Supernatural Organization of Work

The union of work with prayer usually encounters great difficulties. The real difficulty lies in this, that, seen from the outside, there is a certain divergence between prayer and work. Prayer withdraws us from the world, from all that is temporal around us, from all external life, and causes us to become entirely immersed in God. Work, on the other hand, draws us toward creation. In work the world of created things demands our full attention; it insists on our being fully taken up with it. Men usually try to give their work in the temporal world value by devoting themselves completely to it.

Prayer and work both bring us back to God

Is the divergence as wide as we think it is? For does not work lead us toward creation? And in creation the marks of God's hand are to be found. By the will of God, creation is the first witness to Him before man. Indeed, the created world, even without the help of Revelation, would bear witness to God.

If, then, the created world is the first voice of God's Revelation for the human mind, it cannot be otherwise in human work. God addresses us through the created world; in it the reflection of God's beauty is shown. Contact with creation in work is contact with God. And in this aspect of work one meets with prayer. Thus there is no real divergence between them. The divergence that often occurs is rather the result of corrupted human nature, of our weakness, than of the way the world is made.

God so conceived the world that creation, like prayer, brings us back to Him; creation does this indirectly, prayer directly. Of course, prayer is the more wonderful way to God. But if it is joined to work, we reach God in two different ways at once.

We can pray at work by remembering God's presence

This apparent divergence can be removed by conquering the incapacity of our mind and will, particularly by remembering that God's presence always accompanies our work: "Seek His countenance always."[80] "It is in Him that we live, and move, and have our being."[81]

Walking in God's presence, acting and working, we keep our attention fixed on life in God Himself, on God's interior life. The whole of creation is enclosed in God's thought, as is therefore that part, too, in which our daily work is accomplished. Our life is contained in God's life, and our activity is contained in God's activity.

Work does not take us out of this union. For we shall not cease to be either the dwelling place of God or the temple of the Holy Spirit. Work does not deprive us of this guest who has bound up

[80] Ps. 104:4 (RSV = Ps. 105:4).

[81] Acts 17:28.

our existence with His own so closely that it is completely dependent on Him.

We can pray by offering our work to God

This link can be strengthened still more by directing toward God the object of our work. The ways in which we must do this will vary a lot, in accordance with our skill in handling ourselves, our thoughts, attention, and feelings in the course of our work. By the exercise of care, we can ensure that we will worship God not only constantly, but by every separate act of our work.

This will be a continual and real sacrifice (in the true meaning of the word) of oneself and one's work to God. For in every sacrifice there is a consecration to God of time, strength, and some material good. In work there is the sacrifice to God of every moment of our toil; thus there is worship of God through the medium of time.

Our work destroys human strength and our very selves through weariness and the "sweat of our brow." There is no work without the destruction of some strength, just as there is no sacrifice without some destruction. And this is the essential part of the sacrifice of work.

Finally, work involves the sacrifice to God of the fruit of our work, the consecration by love of the finished work. By means of our intention, we "save," so to speak, the fruit of our work from its exclusively temporal fate and we return it to God. And thus the worship of God by sacrifice takes place.

In work we can repeat the words of the Liturgy of the Mass, in reference to ourselves: "We offer Thee, O Lord, the chalice of salvation," the chalice of hardship, toil, and suffering. "Accept, O Holy Father, almighty and eternal God, this spotless Host." The host is the finished work, born of submission and obedience to men and to God. Now, holding the fruit of our work, we stand in the full light of God's countenance. He is the witness of our work. God is no longer distant for us; He comes down into our personal life. There rises up in us a sense of the nearness of the sanctifying God. Even the most absorbing kind of work can be linked with such a surrender of oneself to God.

We can pray at each stage in our work

Besides this method, which is open even to those most given to distraction, there is another, for souls who are exceptionally united to God and who can pray by every act they perform in the course of work. This is a kind of supernatural organization of work: a division of work into a number of little activities, each of which we give back to God in a separate act of love. It is possible to set all the activities of the day into this framework. However, it is sufficient to get through some determined task well once during the course of the day in order to acquire wonderful fruits in the sanctification of the temporal.

For instance, suppose we have been given a set task to perform. We go over the course of action in our mind, the whole process, with all the movements involved: deeds and actions, thoughts and plans, hopes, joys, and fears. In the course of this task we shall, with the help of the rational will, have to join together a series of deliberate actions. What will the worth of this work be? Shall we be able to raise it above the temporal, to sanctify it and ourselves in it, to extend its perspectives as far as the gates of Heaven? Or shall we keep it from ever rising above the earth? Let us make a start, anyway!

First of all, there should be a prayer for the way. Honesty, dutifulness, a need perhaps, a command, or maybe love has laid this work on us. Perhaps it even comes as a surprise to us. We embrace it with our mind, will, and love. Or perhaps with fear and dislike? In the face of this work, all the results of Original Sin peer out of our soul. I give myself more courage and say, "Do ye manfully, and let your heart be strengthened."[82] Perhaps there is revolt and conspiracy in me. What is left to me? "O God, my God, I wait for Thee as for the dawn."[83] See, I am ready! I am here! Slowly the light returns to me.

My work has its own *Introit*. To every task, even the pleasant ones, is joined a certain fear. Maybe at times it is really salutary. How good it is, in the offering of our work, to begin from the *Confiteor:* "I have sinned by my thoughts, words, and deeds." It is all contaminated and aching from sin. "Without Thee I can do nothing."[84] And yet I want to! I long to make reparation by my work — by thought, word, and deed — to wipe out my previous faults! For in every kind of work there is room for thought, word, and deed, and as I have offended God by them, so now I want to make amends to Him in work.

With a feeling of guilt, which may weigh on the course of my work, I ascend — like the priest to the altar — the steps of isolation, bringing my request: "That I may serve Thee with a clear mind in a spirit of concentration and with the purest intentions." This is where we must purify our intentions. A final preparation: "Open my lips, O Lord, that I may bless thy Holy Name."[85]

We have put our hand to the plow; we have set our work in motion. I know that my activity is wholly dependent on God's activity. For there is no human activity without a previous stimulus from God. "My Father has never ceased working, and I, too,

[82] Cf. 2 Kings 13:28 (RSV = 2 Sam. 13:28).

[83] Ps. 62:1 (RSV = Ps. 63:1).

[84] Cf. John 15:5.

[85] *Prayer before reciting the Divine Office.*

must be at work."[86] I know what this means. Every movement, every step, every stirring of our thought, will, or muscle, every contraction of the hand: all this takes place by the power of the Prime Mover, God. We have merely joined ourselves to God's strength, as a lamp, glowing with electric power, is connected to a plug. We have become the shoots of God's vine; we live on in Him. We have to bear fruit.

We pray with the words of *Prime*, that God may assist us with His power, "that all our thoughts, words, and deeds should be directed toward the fulfilment of His justice." Continual watchfulness over the course of our work is enriched by this link with God, by our presence of mind, the control of our feelings, and the ennoblement of our motives.

Our work has its own *Te Deum*. It is drawing to an end. We already have a feeling of joy and worship for God, from whom came "both the will and the deed."[87] Joy in a task completed is a natural thing and man's right. Every newly arisen good awakens joy. We should build a supernatural tower onto this natural joy. "To the one God praise and glory."[88] Give to God what comes from God! The final act of work is the acknowledgment of our impotence and the worship of God's goodness.

This is prayer in the course of work. By taking this way, we can offer to God a year of work, a season, a month, a day, the course of every activity, and particularly the more important ones. Let us allow for our weakness, however. It is better to live properly through one action a day in this way, than to go beyond our psychological possibilities in work. For everyone has his own particular grace given to him.

[86] John 5:17.

[87] Phil. 2:13.

[88] Cf. Ps. 95:7 (RSV = Ps. 96:7).

We can pray in the hardship of our work

Various difficulties, obstacles, failures, opposition, and hardships arise in the course of work. Even though we may enter into work with the best of intentions, its very weight can kill joy within us, disturb our equilibrium, and rob us of peace again and again.

How different a city looks in the early morning, when the crowds of rested, happy people are going to work, from the evening, when the worn-out, drooping figures return, weighed down with the burden of the whole day.

There is prayer in the hardship of work, too. We should arm ourselves against the unexpected that may come to us during work with the spirit of obedience so much praised by the centurion: "I too know what it is to obey authority; I have soldiers under me, and I say, 'Go,' to one man, and he goes, or, 'Come,' to another, and he comes, or, 'Do this,' to my servant, and he does it."[89] Then every unforeseen change, every disruption of our work, and every order that upsets our prearranged plans or the day's schedule will be received in a spirit of supernatural submission. And when difficulties arise in the course of the work itself, we accept them with the conviction that the good God really wishes to deepen our personal relationship to work, for "man is proved in adversity."[90]

"Do ye manfully, and let your heart be strengthened." Encouragement increases our effort. To try and bargain with increasing internal resistance leads to defeat. Determined courage prepares the ground for victory.

When we lack success in work, there is the prayer of humility. We say to ourselves, "We are useless servants."[91] We did not do

[89] Matt. 8:9.

[90] Cf. Prov. 17:17; 2 Cor. 6:4.

[91] Luke 17:10.

what we should have done. Often this little bit of humility is very necessary. A little capacity for being ashamed and humble teaches us prudence, attentiveness, foresight, and caution in our actions. "It is good for me that Thou hast humbled me: that I may learn Thy justifications."[92]

Finally, there is the prayer of hardship, suffering, and sweat. In this toil is the sure remedy for the fruits of Original Sin, and the salvation of one's soul through the burden of work. For this cleansing toil, we should thank God.

These remarks do not indicate the only way to the sanctification of work. In every man it can take a different course. Everyone can solve this union of work and prayer according to his own spiritual capacity. For there are as many different ways of worshipping God, of practicing the asceticism of work, as there are minds and hearts, as there is will and love, and as there are kinds of work and duties. Every one of God's workers can develop his own philosophy of asceticism in work, and the prayer in work that will best answer the needs of his soul.

The pattern laid down here is like the frame in the beehive, which the bee can fill with honey taken from innumerable flowers. Only when one solves for oneself the problem of the form that prayer is to take in one's work, does one begin to realize the importance of the question.

God wants to be adored in these different ways, by each man in his own way. The richness of work-prayer is love. As a result, the time we use in work is imbued with the love of God, by which we sanctify our thoughts, our words, and our deeds.

[92] Ps. 118:71 (RSV = Ps. 119:71).

10

By the Sweat of Your Brow

The plane on which we have been considering work up to this point is so lofty, and the view from that height makes work appear to be so beautiful and colorful, that it can easily come to seem nothing but joy, as well as the highest measure of goodness, grace, and love.

Work mysteriously encompasses joy and pain

To be sure, we derive much joy from work. "It is good to give praise to You, Lord, and to sing to Thy name, O most High. . . . For Thou hast given me, O Lord, a delight in Thy doings and in the works of Thy hands I shall rejoice."[93]

Certainly, we discover both joy and grace in work. But we also meet toil, grief, and suffering there. Even if we raise work from the realm of suffering to the highest degree of supernaturalness, we are not able to lift the whole burden from it, not even by the most

[93] Ps. 91:2, 5 (RSV = Ps. 92:1, 4).

exalted prayer. It is a condition of work itself that it should contain some burden and toil.

In human work we see a mingling of joy and suffering, liberation and dependence. Man toils and at the same time is glad; he surrenders to the heavy law of work and at the same time feels freed from something. In work there is something of the contradiction inherent in man's nature, an echo, as it were, of Paul's complaint: "I observe another disposition in my lower self, which wars against the disposition of my conscience."[94]

This is the mystery! Who will explain it to us? Why is every sort of work, even the most joyful, still so tiresome? Why does even the man best suited to work, the man who loves it above all other temporal happiness, find suffering and pain in it?

The burden of work is the result of sin

In order to clear up this mystery, one must look at it from the viewpoint of faith. Faith teaches us that, before the coming of Original Sin, work was pure joy for man. Toil and hardship were not known to Adam before his sin. Only afterwards did sin add oppressiveness, hardship, sweat, and weariness to work, which was always man's duty. The sentence was pronounced: "Cursed is the earth in thy work; with labor and toil shalt thou eat thereof all the days of thy life. Thorns and thistles shall it bring forth to thee and thou shalt eat the herbs of the earth. By the sweat of thy brow thou shalt eat bread."[95] This is the result of man's disobedience to God!

Work did not lose any of its nobility; it was still indispensable to man as a rational creature. But with work, noble though it still was, there now went dullness and intractability, weighing down all

[94] Rom. 7:23.

[95] Gen. 3:17-19.

labor, both physical and spiritual. And here the pain is all the greater the more necessary the work is. Man knows that he must work, for both his mind and his will tell him so, but he also knows that he cannot satisfy this need without becoming subject, willingly or unwillingly, to the law of suffering.

Work is a rational activity and a virtue. Every act of virtue is difficult, although virtues are alluringly beautiful. Sin made the human mind dull; it made it difficult to know what is good, for merely to understand is a labor. Sometimes one must devote one's whole life in order to understand and define some particle of truth. How tyrannical learning is, what a ruthless mistress, to demand the sacrifice of a whole life! And yet for all the human lives sacrificed, how little we know and learn. This is the result of the darkening of human understanding by sin.

Work is also burdensome from the viewpoint of the human will, for every effort aches from the wounds of Original Sin. There is some suffering lying in wait for us everywhere, and it takes such complete possession of us that we come to fear the slightest effort, lest we reopen our wounds. So we react with inner resistance to even the most attractive work, lest we disturb the sinful habits that the will has acquired.

Because of Original Sin, matter resists man

The fatigue of work also arises out of the fact that, from the very moment of the original sin of Adam, there has prevailed in the world a revolt of nature against man. Matter answers revolt with revolt. Man refused allegiance to God, and, infected by this bad example, the created world stiffened in opposition to man. From the moment when the king of creatures lost his crown of grace, the world has only been subject to him under protest. "The whole of nature, as we know, groans in a common travail all the while."[96] The groans of fallen man reverberate — with an echo increased a hundredfold — throughout nature.

Wherever we look, we see this revolt and suffering. There is the wearisome process of work itself. Almost every sort of work consists of the repetition of a long series of monotonous acts that make up one main activity or produce one result. There are almost no simple acts, complete in themselves: every act is composite, has its own physiology, its own set of actions and movements. And it is just this, the repetition of effort (even though it is a small effort) that is wearisome.

We particularly lack perseverance for monotonous acts that do not have a great individual effect. We can screw ourselves up to great, impressive actions, but it is hard to acquire quiet patience. We are too capable, our intelligence is too quick, we grasp things too easily to renounce ourselves, and to condemn ourselves to such plodding. This is the cause of much of our suffering. Herein lies the painful mystery of work — and its cross.

If we were to go through the whole world, and peep into the dark mines, into the noisy halls full of machines, into the dirty factories, if we were only to pass, in our minds, through these sorrowful places of daily work where people put in eight to twelve hours a day, only then would we come to know the whole pressing burden of work.

It will do no harm to give a few examples, taken from the official reports of a work-inspector. These are the bare facts. But a description is never the reality itself.

Here is a printing house, where a woman is working at a pedal machine — that is, a machine set in motion by movements of the foot. In the course of an eight-hour working day this woman exerts, from a standing position, ninety-six hundred pressures of

[96] Rom. 8:22.

her foot on the pedal, with her arms bent at the elbows all the time, with continually strained attention.

In a brickkiln, the work of the brickmakers (who are women) demands an enormous effort of the hand and of the whole torso, an effort repeated from twelve hundred to three thousand times daily. In the manufacture of bricks, women lift a weight of from twenty-seven to forty pounds through a space of twenty-six to thirty-three feet.

The way in which the spirit of the worker is affected by excessive effort is illustrated by the case of a woman who was attending four looms at the same time — work requiring continual nervous strain. "When she raised her head," described the work-inspector, "she had a completely wild look: her face was sweating so much that it seemed to be drenched with water; her eyes had an expression of extreme dejection, fear, and tiredness. To a question as to how the work was going, she replied with one word: 'Terrible.' "[97]

Sometimes the hygienic conditions of human work are appalling. The workers in a button factory have to wear handkerchiefs over their noses and mouths; otherwise they would be in a continual state of suffocation owing to the clouds of dust. They work without a dinner break; they eat their breakfast during work in the same dust-filled room. It is the same in the factory in which medicinal herbs are sorted, where a thick layer of the extremely penetrating and corrosive dust of the herbs covers everything that is in the workshop even for a few minutes.

One lady work-inspector declares, "It was completely incomprehensible to me how people could work in some parts of a comb and button factory." The air in one of the factories that she saw,

[97] H. Krahelska, M. Kirstowa, St. Wolski, *Ze wspomnien inspektora pracy*, vol. 2 (Warsaw, 1936), 133.

saturated with acetic acid, immediately stopped her breathing. The corrosive acid forced tears from her eyes, although she only watched the work from the doorway of the factory hall.[98]

This is not literature; these are not extracts from descriptions in novels. We are quoting them to show how heavy human work can be, how all the objects of our daily use are bathed in human sweat, pain, and suffering, and how many daily hardships are involved in their manufacture. It is good to remember this.

Great strength is needed if one is to sanctify such work. The examples we have given prove that bad organization adds even more to the usual burden of work. If the Church interests Herself in the problem of the organization of work, it is because She does not want to allow any unnecessary increase in the already wearisome burden of work. And we must think of the soul of the working man; we must remember that he, too, must change, sanctify himself, and confer a salutary and liberating character on his work.

Sin causes us to resist each other

Finally, the burden of work is also increased by the revolt of man against his brother in work.

The effort necessary to cooperate with other people also runs counter to our nature, for sin has closed man up in himself and plunged him into selfishness and pride. Sin has disrupted the social nature of man, turned him away from God and from his neighbor, and steered him toward self-worship, the adoration of himself and of his own mind and will. When this process repeats itself in a different form in every individual, it is easy to see the conflict that life in common can entail.

[98] Ibid., vol. 1, 224.

The man who gives the orders for work, the man who supervises it, and the man who performs it, will all bring divergent thoughts and wills to the one activity. How difficult is the adjustment of activities here, even with the exercise of good will! And what happens when it is lacking? The greater the desolation wrought by sin in the soul, the harder it is to achieve harmony.

But does not work require one to forget oneself, to give oneself to others, and to surrender oneself? This awakens horror in man. Sin, having conquered man, guards its inheritance, lest man be snatched away by grace. A struggle begins with grace and with all those who prepare the way for it — even though it is only through work that we will be freed from this struggle.

Christian hope sees the toil of work as salvific

We have to keep this sad reality under control, to rule and conquer it. But how?

In every hardship, in every pain, we should perceive the mystery of man's liberation. The Christian attitude to the toil of work consists in this — that we wish to confer a saving character on this residue of suffering that cannot be eliminated even by the just organization of work. Christian thought awakens a little joy, hope, and confidence here also.

The heaviest work, the most wearisome bustle, and all the suffering arising out of it: these things are not fruitless, even if they have been exploited by the most inhuman businessmen.

Our rational nature has a right and a duty to see to it that the burden of work should be lightened. Businessmen, directors, and organizers of work have a moral obligation to arrange the condition of work so that it will be worthy of man.

But when everything possible has been done, when conscientiousness, reason, and good will have come into play, the toil of work will still remain — and we ought to give it back to God with the same intention with which God demands the "sweat of our brow" in atonement for our revolt.

Man cannot desire complete liberation from the hardship of work, for that hardship frees him from sin. And we offer the whole pain of work to God through Christ who invites us: "Come to me, all you who labor and are burdened; I will give you rest."[99]

[99] Matt. 11:28.

11

The Mystery of Redemption in Work

In a well-organized life there are no "leftovers" in the sense of superfluous actions and superfluous time. Nothing can be wasted, nothing let go. We cannot pass over any opportunity through which the seed of grace and of salvation may increase in us.

Every man has a duty to be a good husbandman of his vineyard, and the good farmer sees to it that every plant bears fruit.

We cannot afford the sort of work that will not bear fruit a hundredfold. But hundredfold fruit is the fruit of grace, of holiness, and of the union of the soul with God. This is the whole economy of our life's toil.

The toil of daily work is not hopeless. It can become the medicine of corrupted human nature. With the help of toil, we can struggle against the corruption brought about in us both by Original Sin and by our own sins.

Every sin makes the work of the mind and will more difficult; it destroys something of their efficiency. Work sets out to repair this loss of efficiency, and to obliterate the traces of sin. In all work we see the lines of this struggle: we try to conquer ourselves, to use violence on ourselves and on our slowness, lack of will, listlessness, and weakness. Man, when he is forced by work to break with selfishness, frees himself from the flaws and consequences of sin and prepares the terrain for virtues.

Work should ennoble the worker

We deduce from this that the toil of work can be ennobling: by itself it cannot degrade man. Only badly organized work, or injustice in the way it is regulated — the crushing burden of work beyond human endurance — can degrade man. It is then that the revolt of the world of work is born, the revolt of the workers, and the social revolt against the degradation of man in work. As Pius XI said, this is a just revolt, that man might not emerge coarsened and vulgarized from the workshop where dead matter is being ennobled.[100] Here there is an obvious abuse that cries to Heaven for vengeance, for it wrecks God's saving plan in relation to work. If, however, a just measure is observed, then every sort of work can and ought to ennoble.

In every resistance we meet in work, we recognize man's resistance to God. The effort with which man acts on matter and ennobles it is like God's effort when He acts on man to ennoble him. God is continually correcting His work in us, wishing to stamp His image, the light of His countenance on it. Similarly man leaves his mark on the object of his work. From the work we recognize the master. However, in this action of man on matter, we come up against the resistance of matter, which is like the resistance of man to God.

Matter yields in the end, however, to the human mind and will, and this surrender should serve to encourage the surrender of man

[100]Pius XI, *Quadragesimo Anno*, section 153.

to God. As clay yields to the potter, so man yields to God; as the hardest rock yields to the sculptor who deals it good, painful blows, yet ennobles it, giving it beauty of form — the stamp of his genius — so man, however much tried by God, once he has yielded to Him, emerges from every trial more similar to the image of God.

The example of liberated matter inclines us toward this surrender to God, for we see how matter immediately runs wild whenever it escapes from the guiding human hand. We see how blind nature avenges itself on the civilization that ennobles it and on human work, burying it in the ruin of prehistory. Krasinski saw in the Roman Forum, protruding from mountains of rubbish and ruins, the capitals of what had once been the columns of glorious temples. How great a desolation the freedom of blind strength can bring about! In Crete the remains of wonderful cities have been dug up — traces of a prehistoric Aegean civilization that may have been richer than the Greek or Roman. And it all lies in ruins.

We are witnesses of the struggle with the rock in the quarries, with the stony soil, with the bare crags. We see the onrush of the desert overwhelming human settlements as soon as irrigation is neglected. The raging flood mocks human barriers. All of this cries out to man, "I will not serve."[101] And yet it does serve.

When man begins to serve God, when he himself is frightened by the terrifying picture of the ruin wrought in the soul by revolt, he comes to hate this desolation. In the ruins of creation man sees the image of the havoc created in the soul that has rebelled. Today, when bombed towns lie shattered in ruins, it is obvious that this is the work of hate and not of virtue and labor. Man comes to his senses. "I will arise and go to my father."[102] Here is one more motive that should encourage us to ennoble our souls by work.

[101] Jer. 2:20.
[102] Luke 15:18.

And what else? Work, by its difficulty, redeems, liberates, ennobles, and sanctifies.

Work wears away our physical strength and uses up some of its reserves. In this way it frees our spirit from the domination of matter and of the body. Man becomes the borderline between the earthly world and the heavenly. Work only develops the physical and spiritual skills of man to certain limits: when they are developed to the peak of their possibilities, they begin to give out. A lifetime of work leaves its mark on us. Hard work frees us gradually from the body and its powers; by tiring the body, it calms it down and makes it easier for us to exercise control over it.

What is more, by wearisome work man repays to God the debts incurred by sin. How often we forget this! If the labor of work is accepted with love, this work of redemption by toil will bring us to the gates of merit. For work must be carried out not only for temporal good, but for eternal. Work comprises not only the task of life on earth, but also the task of eternal life.

"By the sweat of thy brow shalt thou eat bread until thou return to the earth, out of which thou wast taken," until the very instant that the union of Heaven and earth takes place.

And so work is not merely the fulfilment of our vow of obedience or of our profession, nor is it merely the voice of duty or of the needs of our stomach. The whole hardship of work is disproportionately great in comparison with these aims. The sweat of a man's toil-stained face marks a suffering that purifies not so much the body as the soul. In this suffering is the whole Calvary of man, who dies every day on the cross of his life in order to destroy death by this slow death-agony, and so to attain the glory of resurrection. Man, bathed in sweat, knows that there is no earthly reward, no wages or recompense, that could ever pay him enough for this sacrifice. The hard workers can always ask, "How is a man the better for it, if he gains the whole world at the expense of losing his soul?"[103] What would come of the most productive, tiring work by miners in the earth, or by workers in factories, slaving away in constant terror of bombs; what would come of all this work, if it did not contain in itself a task for eternal life? When, in the suffering work entails, we see these tasks of eternity, this pledge of the soul's ransom, a change comes over even the weariest.

For it is in such toil that we discover the value of suffering. The toil of work for us will be this everyday, familiar cross: suffering toward which we hasten, suffering that is not, indeed, as sublime as that which hagiography describes but which is no less real, precious, and full of merit.

For in such toil we discover the value of patience. We know that we are not struggling only for the temporal perfection of our work, or for mere profit or gain, but for eternal perfection, for the eternal fruits of ordinary, everyday work.

For in such toil we discover satisfaction for our faults, from which no child of earth is free. Toil, accepted in a proper spirit, is for us an anticipation of Purgatory. It is possible for us here below to sweat the stains of sin, our whole responsibility for our faults, out of our system by means of work, and to give them back to the earth from which we took our sins. This is the extraordinary dispensation of time.

Work is an instrument of salvation

It can be seen from this that work is not the curse of man and that toil is not humiliating, for it contains hope. The sweat of one's brow and the labor of one's hands do not debase; they raise up and exalt. Work becomes an instrument, one of the means of salvation. The toil of work is linked with the joy of victory over matter and

[103]Matt. 16:26; Luke 9:25.

over oneself. It is therefore a double joy. To the natural joy of a new task completed there is added a supernatural joy that the work is, in every respect, well done, since it brings us even further on our road to eternal life.

The sight of a man hard at work is full of consolation. We say to ourselves, "By the sweat of his brow our brother is saving his soul." Let us yearn to support him, to lift up his cross with the arms of the Cyrenian.[104] The act of salvation is taking place. Let us hasten with help, that the yield may be a hundredfold. These are the most important thoughts bearing on the problem of the redemptive toil of human work.

A few conclusions arise out of this. It is under the excessive burden of work, surpassing human endurance, that man most often breaks down. But even if this excessive toil produced no other fruit than the feeling of our weakness, our lack of skill and strength, it would still not be wasted. If in excessive work we recognize our helplessness, and from it learn humility in relation to God and full dependence on Him, it is already much!

In view of the truth that toil is satisfaction for our faults, we have a duty to offer our suffering and sweat to God. Not only is work laid down by God, but the very hardship it involves has its allotted task. We must guide it, therefore, toward its redemptive destiny.

We must also offer God the work of those who in their labor think neither of Him nor of the supernatural value of work. Let us glance around at the people working near us. Which of them ever thinks that his work is satisfaction for sin? We must make good their failure to offer it.

And we must also offer God the pain and labor of those who curse the work appointed by God, who rail at both the work and

[104]Cf. Mark 15:21.

God. And there are many like that: not merely individuals, but whole doctrines, whole systems of thought. They curse God and Adam because man wears himself out at work, for they cannot distinguish God's intention from bad human arrangements. Who will take up the toil that they have wasted?

In addition there is the whole multitude of people who make instruments of sin for themselves out of the blessed fruit of hard work, so that, instead of worship resulting from their toil, an insult is offered to God.

Here is the opportunity for beautiful, lofty apostolic work! Christ wants us to place the whole burden of our work on His Cross, to become co-sufferers with Him. The hardship of work is our daily cross. "If anyone wishes to come after me, let him deny himself, and take up his cross, and follow me."[105]

Let us ask ourselves now whether the toil of work is a curse or a punishment, or whether it is yet another lifeline, an opportunity of increasing redemptive grace in oneself? Should we then want work that has been made too easy, comfortable work, work that has been completely purged of all hardship? Would the result not be that that which spared a part of man, ended by impoverishing the whole man? We will obtain full redemption only from Christ: "Come to me all you who labor and are burdened; I will give you rest."[106]

[105]Matt. 16:24; Mark 8:34; Luke 9:23.

[106]Matt. 11:28.

12

The Interior Life and Excessive Work

Daily work has as its aim not merely our purification from the guilt of sin, nor just atonement to God; it must also contribute in its own sphere to the formation of a certain knowledge, certain virtues in the soul, and certain values of the spiritual life. In a word, it is a question of a special asceticism of our daily work.

Certainly, the set of truths considered so far already creates an asceticism of work. Here, however, it is a question of something more, of bringing these principles to life by means of the will working in cooperation with God's grace.

No external, physical, social, or educational work frees us from the need for spiritual work. The new duty, added to those that have gone before, cannot lessen the resources of our interior life.

The spiritual structure of our daily work is well illustrated in Christ's parable of the vine and the branches. In every shoot certain changes can be seen: there is growth, development, and the bearing of fruit. However, these external phenomena are the consequence of an inner process that takes place in the vine. All life is an interior process.

Similarly every activity has its interior process. The fruit of work is tangible externally (for example, the branch bearing its grapes) but the interior life of our work, that which comes from "the abundance of our heart,"[107] cannot be apprehended by the senses. Yet this process of interior activity must exist, for without it our work will not produce any results.

Thus inner activity has its own laws in relation to external work, and one cannot afford to lose sight of these laws. The first of them is as follows.

Interior life is the basis of exterior life

Interior life is the basis of exterior life and of all physical, educational, social, and scientific work. The starting point for every kind of work ought to be the interior life, just as the branch comes forth from the life of the vine itself.

And here indeed one has to combine all the truths that create the Christian outlook on work. They must all be experienced by us, not only in relation to their inner depth, but also in relation to the meaning they hold for our work.

Thus we ought to have in our work a consciousness of God's sovereignty over every sort of work: of the fact that God is the beginning and the end of every action, and therefore also of external actions.

We ought to have Christ's redemptive work before our eyes, that activity that raises our external acts (even those that are purely temporal) to a spiritual level and gives them a higher character and value. Otherwise daily work will be purely natural and pagan; the real strength that is to be found in all work done by a man who is living with God, will not be in it. From Christ's

[107] Cf. Matt. 12:34; Luke 6:45.

redemptive work flows our whole knowledge of grace and of God's share in man's activity. It is necessary to keep it before the mind's eye in every sort of work, if that work is to acquire depth and to have a sure foundation. In every kind of work there must be a drawing on Christ: "In Him is life."[108] To manifest Him can be both our natural and our supernatural work. Without either one or the other there is no really fruitful work.

From this follows the second law.

Works of the spirit must come before other works

We have in mind the spirituality of our external work, the primacy of the spirit over action and over matter.

This is an extremely important command, especially today. Indeed, we talk a great deal about social-religious work and often forget that it is impossible to "help God" in the regeneration of the world without first calling on His help. For there is no shortage of people of good will, animated by the love of God and the Church and by concern for the kingdom of God on earth, who want to renew the world but are themselves old and dead in spirit. There is no shortage of religious workers who feel Martha's anxiety about the fate of God in the world, but who forget about the fate of God in their own souls. We can at times be struck down by this illness, this illusion, when we show great zeal over our everyday work, losing the consciousness that the "works of the spirit" ought to take precedence over the other means of action available to us.

For is it not a question of the whole spirituality of our exterior work, that it should not be understood in a wholly material sense? And especially that the work undertaken in the field of religion for the glory of God, should not be infected with the world? The

[108]Cf. John 1:4.

danger of such infection threatens when we have used all the means available but have forgotten that we cannot help God without God's own help, that we cannot conduct any activity unless there is a link with Him who is the source of all strength.

"It is the spirit that quickens, the body adds nothing."[109] Every work must have some element of the spirit in it. The body is dead matter if the spirit does not breathe power into human muscles. "Only those who welcomed Him, He empowered to become the children of God, all those who believe in His name."[110]

And so in all our work, even our physical work, the Holy Spirit must reign, who will stimulate us to action and give to our work a new force and meaning. And only then shall we realize "that it was through Him that all things came into being, and without Him came nothing that has come to be."[111]

This is the "law of spirituality" of human work. The third law comes directly from it.

Work's external fruits depend on interior life

Here, of course, we have in mind work that is Christian in the full meaning of that word: work, namely, that achieves all the goals appointed to human work by God.

In order to achieve them, we must have interior life. Otherwise what we do — particularly in the social, religious, or apostolic field — will be a caricature of work, and will be as much a waste of God's energy as is the waste of badly used nourishment. For such work does not make use of all the values that God wants to get out of our work. Even temporal work, conducted on supernatural

[109]John 6:64.
[110]John 1:12.
[111]John 1:3.

principles, demands the existence of interior life for its full fruitfulness. "Whoever lives in me and I in him, will yield much fruit."[112] Only such work can change us inwardly.

Any neglect in our interior life because of too much work is reflected in the quality of our work, for the lack of personal virtue becomes visible in it, and this lack can bring all our acts to nothing. The most attractive ideas will not help then; if the link between the interior life and the active disappears, the act being performed will fail, as so many acts have failed. The history of the various religious orders has plenty to teach us on this question.

On the other hand, the union of these two paths leading to one act forms in us — with the help of work — virtues that are very useful and fruitful in personal work, and all the more so in collective work.

In our usual daily business we sometimes recognize a springlike breath of joy in work that is suddenly going "like a house on fire." What is happening? Maybe our prayers have gone better? Or maybe God has smiled on us more expressively and we were able to catch that smile: hence this joy and cheerfulness in our work, creating an atmosphere of readiness and ease of cooperation. It is certainly impossible not to appreciate the needs of human nature, which can express themselves in daily suffering. But there is always "the Spirit that quickens."

From these laws it is easy to deduce the fourth.

Active work does not excuse neglect of the interior life

It sometimes happens that our spiritual activities suffer because of too much work dictated by the love of our neighbor. But this sad necessity must not become the rule. Every type of active work is a

[112]John 15:5.

duty added to one that already exists, which ought to be preserved in its entirety.

Active work demands even more watchfulness and concentration on the interior life. This is the problem that presented itself to Cardinal Ferrari in his essentially social work; the numerous apostolic tasks that scattered the members of the Society of St. Paul seemed to multiply endlessly under his very eyes. He understood then that, if one is to fulfil one's duties, one has to have the help of the Spirit of God, and that it is vital to rearrange one's occupations in such a way that it is never necessary to drop prayer. And so the members of the Society filled all their wanderings through the streets and all their journeys by bus and train with prayer. In this way they strove to rescue their interior life from the avalanche of apostolic work.

"For the mouth speaks from the abundance of the heart."[113] Active work must be the manifestation of the interior life and not vice versa. It is only what we have thought and prayed over that we can give to others.

These are the "laws" that must regulate our active life. Ordinary everyday work leads us to prayer, and to union with God. The more this work absorbs us, the closer to God it should be.

Social groups must balance interior life and exterior work

It is the same in social activity. A group of a social character, devoted to active work, is something more than a contemplative order. Greater demands are made on it. For although the contemplative order retains its precedence, the duties of the members of social groups are greater. While maintaining unity with God, they must also worship Him by serving their neighbors. This is a

[113]Matt. 12:34; Luke 6:45.

difficult problem but is, at the moment, particularly apposite. The times are tough and demand the fulfilment of exceptional tasks: of warmer love of God and more active love of one's neighbor. Once again the problem of interior life has to be solved. This is no longer the problem of "Martha or Mary" but the problem of "Mary in Martha." We solve it in active daily work — "for the mouth speaks from the abundance of the heart."

We solve it by fulfilling Christ's command: "Let your light shine before men that they may see your good works and glorify your Father."[114]

[114]Matt. 5:16.

13

The Spiritual and Social Values of Work

Laws that link the interior with the active life, point to the existence of a joyous interdependence between them, between, as it were, the "Martha" and "Mary" in us. Here, too, is certainly a reflection of the light of God's Incarnation, the eternal motif by which God regulates His relations with the world: the Incarnation of the Son of God into a body taken from this earth, the incarnation of a soul into matter, the incarnation of interior life into external life. Here also is the link between grace and nature, which comes from God's hands that it may be the handmaid of the Word Incarnate who lives in our midst.

In what does this joyous helpfulness consist? One might express it in these words: the interior life supplies the active life with virtues and skills, and the active, working life tests these values in the fire of work.

Let us clarify this a bit. The interior life is the school of all the virtues and therefore also of the social "working virtues" — those virtues that share in the process of human work in a special manner. And which of them does not share in this process?

Work presupposes faith of some kind

By means of interior life we acquire above all a warm and living faith, not in the sense that this life is the origin of faith, but that our faith is enkindled through our interior life.

Is there any connection between this and work? It is obvious that without some faith, without faith "in something," it is hard to arouse any sort of enthusiasm in oneself. The higher and more wonderful the object of this faith is, the higher and greater is our enthusiasm for action. Every man who wishes to do something in life tries to acquire some ideal, purpose, or faith: there is no lack of examples today. People who have ceased to believe in God look for faith in man, the world, matter, good economics, or class, in order that they may not be left without any ideal at all. Do not all these contemporary tendencies, in the name of which people go to so much trouble, seem to be based on some kind of faith?

If, then, some ideal is needed in the purely natural order in order to acquire material goods, all the more is it needed in the sort of work that links temporal aims with eternal work that should have a supernatural character.

Interior life cultivates the virtues needed for work

With interior life we acquire, in addition, charity toward God, which we express in work for our neighbor and which is an indispensable virtue in all work. It can be seen from our considerations about the social value of work how important this acquisition is. Besides, does not all love have its origins in God's love?

Moreover, with interior life we acquire deep humility. Every person who, with the help of God's grace, has honestly sifted his soul to the bottom, knows that every victory over himself is born from the mustard seed of humility. Is not this lesson repeated *ad infinitum* within us? Humility is the mother of the foremost qualities, merits, and virtues. It teaches us circumspection in activity, caution, thoroughness, conscientiousness, and faithfulness. The virtues that we have acquired will shine through our deeds and all their merits will be reflected in the work we do.

But such unusual and important virtues as calm, supernatural peace, moderation, and Christian patience — all of these spring from interior life. This is the contribution the supernatural life has to make to the active, external social life.

There is, however, something more to be said.

Exterior work reveals our virtues and defects

Without external work we could not know ourselves fully, for only in daily work do we have a perfect opportunity to observe ourselves; it is then indeed that we discover the good and evil in ourselves, and see our merits and faults. Without active work it is usually very hard to know oneself, for there is a lot of hidden evil in us, covered over with apparent calm.

What external work does for our interior life is shown in the fact that this work by the sweat of our brow lays bare the image of our soul and unveils its real expression.

And how easy it is to overlook this! Even in our daily examination of conscience we do not pay much heed to the manner in which we inwardly accept the difficulties of the day. We hardly ever look at the work we have done from the point of view of the internal process that took place within us as we did it. Which can be seen in it: thoroughness or superficiality, the control of our feelings or the unchecked action of instincts and emotions? A perfect method of examining our conscience can be to scrutinize the manner in which we do our duty at work. It is good in examining our day to observe one particular activity, the hardest, the one that forces on us the thing that we do not like, or the activity that has fallen to us unexpectedly. In this mirror we shall perceive the spirit that governs us in reality.

This is what we call the joyous helpfulness, or mutual aid, between interior life and external life.

Interior life gives us a social spirit

The life of work receives yet another good from interior life: this is that our soul becomes more aware of others, which is an indispensable condition for the fruitfulness of active work. For, as we must remind ourselves, every sort of work in cooperation is work with others; it cannot flourish unless we have some social inclination, some ease of manner, some capacity and readiness for meeting our neighbor halfway. If we are to attain this disposition, we must, by means of the supernatural life, uproot all excessive individualism within ourselves — all our self-centered tendencies and everything that makes us overrate our personal worth, detrimental as these failings are to the social values that bring us closer to people.

The supernatural life introduces into our soul equilibrium between the personal character and the social one. When this is done, man draws close to the ideal of perfection and to the harmony of goals and powers. When selfishness and egoism disappear in us, God (and in Him, our neighbor) becomes the center of our action and intentions. Only then are we capable of going outside ourselves and of cooperating with others.

Interior life helps balance prudence and enthusiasm

When our interior life makes us more socially minded, we become able to integrate the efforts of our mind, will, and feelings in our work. The lack of such integration in work leads to continual conflicts between superiors and subordinates, between old and young. The old, being more experienced, are more apt to be guided by prudence; reflection plays a greater part in their work, which leads to a certain slowness of action. The young, on the other hand, tend to identify will with reason, desire with performance.

The conflict between the so-called old and young has been intensified lately by slogans such as "The young are on the march, make way for the young," and "We want something new." These ought to be phrased differently where work is concerned: "We want something *good*." If, indeed, we do want something new, it should not destroy the good that has already been achieved.

In his Christmas message for 1942 Pius XII most properly drew attention to the link that ought to exist in work between the experience of the old and the will to work of the young.

If they are not employed — as they should be — in the service of the good under unsullied standards, enthusiasm and courage are not enough. Unless they are based on God and His eternal truth, all struggle, toil, and labor are in vain:

> When mature men and young men, while remaining always at anchor in the sea of the eternally active tranquillity of God, coordinate their differences of temperament and activity in a genuine Christian spirit, then if the propelling element is joined to the refraining element, the natural differences between the generations will never become dangerous, and will even conduce vigorously to the enforcement of the eternal laws of God in the changing course of times and of conditions of life.[115]

[115] Pius XII, "The Internal Order of States and People." English translation in *The Catholic Mind* 41 (January 1943): 52.

The younger generation unfailingly brings fresh strength and impetus to any activity, as well as values that are often enlivening and blessed. However, these must be united with reflection and prudence. Only then will new ideas enrich the values already achieved by the old. When taking over the burden of work from somebody else, we must above all realize the good that has already been done, and the merits of our predecessor that are apparent in his work. Once we know and estimate them at their true value we are free to assess, cautiously, humbly, and tactfully, their shortcomings, and to consider how to correct them, while still retaining our respect for those who worked there without renown, without arrogance or complaint, almost unobserved. It is here that the life and Spirit of God are revealed in us; it is here that we shall give proof of a soul really in touch with others.

Interior life harmonizes superiors and subordinates

There is one more difficulty, the solution to which can be worked out with the help of interior life: namely, the problem of the relationship between superiors and subordinates, between the director and the directed agent. This problem demands great subtlety, something that can only be achieved by living a deeply spiritual life.

St. Paul gives us a principle that can act as a perfect check on a person's fitness and capacity for directive work. "If a man has not learned how to manage his own household, will he know how to govern God's Church?"[116]

Direction over others has to start with direction over oneself, one's own house. A person who possesses the capacity for ruling himself acquires circumspection and caution in his estimate of

[116] 1 Tim. 3:5.

others. Intolerance and hasty judgments of others, the tendency to make people's faults worse than they are: these are usually characteristics of the young. They may also be a sign that one's own personal work has not gone deep enough. Those who have had experience of the hard struggle with themselves are usually cautious; they look at the world with a fatherly eye, for they have already "given life" and they know how hard it comes. In this way they acquire the wisdom needed by those who govern others. God usually gives a hard and laborious interior life to people whom He wishes to train as rulers of others. At this cost He prepares wise instruments of His activity in the souls of our brothers.

Interior life gives us knowledge of people

The wisdom we acquire in spiritual work gives us one great talent: the knowledge of people. We acquire it by the thorough knowledge of self, of the various states of soul that we see in ourselves in the changeable colors of a long-sustained effort of spiritual work. It is not surprising that the knowledge of people is usually an attribute of the old, of those who already possess the virtue above all virtues — prudence.

This is no small contribution of the interior life to the spirit of daily work. This contribution shows that there cannot be a division between the lives of Mary and Martha. They are two sisters, each of whom serves, in her own way, the living Christ in our soul and in the souls of our brothers.

14

Patience in Work

There are various virtues that are connected with work, for the whole man participates in it with all his abilities, his faults, and his merits. All of these are expressed in the course of human work and in its fruits.

Man will see in work, as in a mirror, the reflection of his own worth, for it is in work that we come to know it. The creator is reflected in creation. In work, therefore, we see reflected our love for our neighbor, our meekness and obedience, our humility, disinterestedness, spirit of contemplation, conscientiousness, and prudence.

But there is a special group of virtues, which might be called "the virtues of work" because they are seen most clearly in work and because they are so necessary that without them it would be difficult to perform any work at all. These virtues are *patience* and connected with it *longanimity* or forbearance; in addition, there are *perseverance* and, akin to it, *constancy*, *mildness*, as well as *conscientiousness*. A few words should be devoted to each of these virtues in turn.

First of all is patience. It has its own great part in work, which is as great as that of the virtue of perseverance. However, the function of patience is rather to prepare man for work, while perseverance accompanies it.

Patience differs from constancy and perseverance

Patience does not belong to the cardinal virtues, although it is related to the virtue of fortitude. It is with the help of patience that we are able to endure the evil done to us by others and that we shield ourselves from harmful sorrow.

The evil that we must combat in our work may come from other people, from external circumstances, or from the very factors that make up the process of work. The evil that brings sadness consists of the difficulties and resistance arising out of matter and of the nature of our work, as well as from the people working with us; it also consists in the resistance arising out of our nature, reason, will, and emotions.

But none of these contrarieties is the object of the virtue of patience; the struggle with them is more the concern of the virtues of perseverance and constancy. Patience, on the other hand, has to deal with the sorrow resulting from these contrarieties. The difficulties will usually remain; it is simply impossible for us to rid our work of them.

If these difficulties are due to the fact that work demands a long series of activities, then we will call on perseverance for help. If in the course of work we encounter various failures and obstacles, we will have recourse to the virtue of constancy, which is our most faithful ally in the struggle with our difficulties. Patience, on the other hand, will exist side-by-side with them, but it will not be able to exist alongside sadness. Either patience or sadness! Where sadness reigns, there is no patience.

Patience diminishes the sadness arising from work

Patience plays a great part in work. It has more than once been called "the source and guardian of the virtues"; it is often considered the greatest among them. The importance of patience in spiritual work is that it removes from our soul and inner nature that which stands in the way of the formation, development, and preservation of the virtues. Hence it is so important that, without it, one cannot keep to the path of the virtues, even though their point of departure is love and the grace of God.

The task of patience in work will be to control excessive and undisciplined sadness. This obviously has nothing in common with the salutary sorrow that arises from the loss of supernatural gifts that help us to attain salvation. For such sorrow is indispensable, particularly when it is moderate and united to hope in the goodness of God.

We are speaking here rather of that sadness that so eats into work that it becomes an obstacle to the achievement of a great many good things that constitute the fruits and joys of work. This sadness engenders discouragement. Under its influence people (no matter what their work, even if it was begun with enthusiasm) give way after some time to a state of depression, finding out a thousand "buts," tiny obstacles by which they often justify the lack of results in their work. They are trying not so much to combat the sadness in themselves, as to justify their "buts." They are people who are full of complaints, grievances, and lamentations arising out of their state of sadness. Where such sadness is entertained, work is not joy; it represents rather the performance of a duty, getting drudgery over and done with.

One usually finds joined to this sadness the desire for different work. "How much better that would suit me! I would really work with enthusiasm at that job!" But once we have gotten the job for which we were longing, we soon discover that the sadness has returned, because it was not the work itself that caused it, but something deeper; the real root of this sadness is the lack of patience and the divided attention, whose result is that "our works are not full."[117]

From such a state of affairs, other misfortunes follow: our work lacks exactness, conscientiousness, faithfulness, and joy. Such a state usually has a sense of grievance mixed up with it; there is procrastination and waste of time. Work is regarded not so much in the light of the rational will to work as in the shadow of depressing sadness. Such a state, when it overwhelms a man, often destroys the whole worth of his work.

The Bible often warns against such sadness: "Give not up thy soul to sadness, and afflict not thyself in thy own counsel. . . . Have pity on thy own soul, pleasing God, and contain thyself. Gather up thy heart in His holiness: and drive away sadness far from thee. For sadness hath killed many, and there is no profit in it."[118]

Indeed, such a state can be seen very often in souls that have given way to sadness in work — a sadness that very frequently develops into a persecution complex, precisely over the work assigned to them.

God's wisdom gives us the means to combat this agonizing condition: to give ourselves to God and to try to overcome ourselves. For sadness is fruitless and unproductive. It fritters away a great deal of valuable time in empty brooding and "thoughtless thoughts"[119] that rarely lead us to any conclusion, decision, or solution. In the end, we do not know ourselves what it is really all about. The book of Proverbs illustrates this picturesquely: "As a

[117]Cf. Rev. 3:2.

[118]Ecclus. 30:22-25 (RSV = Sirach 30:21-23).

[119]Cf. Isa. 59:7.

moth doth by a garment, and a worm by the wood: so the sadness of a man consumeth the heart."[120]

We must fight such sadness (which is often caused by disappointments in work) with patience. "Happy is he that hath had no sadness in his mind, and who is not fallen from his hope."[121]

Scripture calls us to patience in work

Sacred Scripture not only warns us against sadness but calls us explicitly to patience: "For patience is necessary to you; that, doing the will of God, you may receive the promise."[122] St. Paul recommends it to us in the performance of our daily duties as a school in which we acquire the wisdom of life. "And not only so [do we hope for glory]; but we glory also in tribulations, knowing that tribulation worketh patience; and patience trial; and trial hope; and hope confoundeth not."[123]

Here is a ladder, as it were, by which we go ever higher in all our ordinary, daily work. The oppressive nature of our work, when understood correctly, gives rise to patience, and with patience goes extraordinary wisdom; it teaches us to treat as we should the people and things given to us to work with. The more experience (born of patience) that we possess, the more easily our work goes; from this comes hope, which in its turn engenders the spirit of happiness. Man comes out the winner, even though he has not yet reached the pinnacle of his achievements. "In your patience you shall possess your souls."[124]

[120]Prov. 25:20.

[121]Ecclus. 14:2 (RSV = Sirach 14:2).

[122]Heb. 10:36.

[123]Rom. 5:3-5.

[124]Luke 21:19.

Exactly, in patience! For in daily work we shape and develop ourselves in different ways; the disquieting impulses and tendencies in us are destroyed and through this purification our soul becomes our own. "In your patience you shall possess your souls." Patience leads us to God's supernatural wisdom.

There is a saying that offers a clue to this problem: "A man has as much wisdom as he has patience." Patience is a "political virtue"; it is the skill with the help of which we must organize our own work and that of others.

Patience makes us better workers

Here we recognize the great utility of the virtue of patience. Work is certainly hard enough on its own, but when sadness is added to it, the burden is all the heavier. An impatient man tires himself out more and for longer at work: not only does he suffer from the toil itself but from his own impatience and the sadness that goes with it. Indeed, it is not so much the burden of work this man suffers from as the burden of impatience. On the other hand, a man with self-control does the work entrusted to him far more quickly and easily.

Work done in a spirit of sadness has yet another bad result: the loss of moral fruit and of supernatural merit. The toil involved in such work no longer has the character of redemption and atonement, but is really "toil by the sweat of one's brow," in grief and pain. Going through one's daily occupations in such pain one can truly ask with Ecclesiastes, "What gain has the worker from his toil?"[125] One takes a lot of pains, but everything shows itself to be "vanity of vanities."[126]

[125]Eccles. 3:9.
[126]Eccles. 1:2.

To prevent such an unfortunate result of our work, we must conquer sadness by supernatural motives. Impatience must be overcome by the love of our neighbor. It is not usually inner hostility that warps this love, but impatience. Still, this is not the most important motive in the struggle with sadness. It is more important to realize that patience in work brings results both in this world and in the life to come: in this world, by way of atonement for the sins we have committed; in the next, by the glorious crowning of life's labors.

When we have before our eyes the patience of those around us, the patience of the saints and of the Good Shepherd, Christ our Lord, we gain new strength for the fight. The wanderings of Christ in search of souls throughout the length and breadth of the Holy Land: this is the outstanding example of patience.

The patience of the heavenly Father, as He wins souls for Heaven, and struggles with man for man's happiness, should also be a considerable encouragement to us, that from anguish we may attain patience, from patience, experience, and from experience, hope; for hope does not deceive. "In patience you shall possess your souls."

15

The Virtue of Longanimity in Work

To speak today of the virtue of longanimity is almost demoralizing. Such at least is our first impression, but in the end we shall see this virtue as an inspiration.

What is longanimity? Listing the gifts of the Holy Spirit, the apostle Paul says: "But the fruit of the Spirit is, charity, joy, peace, patience, kindness, goodness, longanimity, mildness, faith, modesty, continence, and chastity."[127] Longanimity appears alongside charity, which "is poured forth in our hearts, by the Holy Spirit, who is given to us."[128] It appears beside joy and peace, which are connected with charity; it is linked with patience. Longanimity is the virtue of forbearance or long-suffering. In a word, it appears in the company of the virtues that avoid disorder, inner disturbance, or dissipation.

Longanimity is the virtue by which we acquire a spirit of lasting endeavor in the pursuit of a distant good; it is the virtue that helps

[127]Gal. 5:22-23.

[128]Rom. 5:5.

us to bear the contrarieties arising from the fact that the good that we have in view can only be achieved after much time and effort.

In this case, endurance is not something to be recommended, but something required. In setting about some work, we see some good in its final outcome. In order to achieve this good, however, great effort and toil are needed.

Consciousness of the distant goal of our endeavor gives rise in us to a peculiar feeling akin to sadness. We must accept the distant goal wholeheartedly, along with the prospect of protracted effort. Faced by this lengthening perspective, man sometimes breaks down in his work.

Longanimity enables us to bear protracted labor

A certain link exists between longanimity and patience. Patience, if it is to achieve the good that is the object of work, has to deal with the sadness that accompanies the work. The shorter the time the work itself lasts, the easier it is to endure the bad side of it. It becomes harder when the good is put off into eternity. Here another difficulty is added to work. Patience does battle with every kind of sadness arising from the toil inherent in work. But in protracted work we must call on the aid of longanimity. Patience protects the mind from the disturbances caused by the evil that threatens in work; it is the task of longanimity, on the other hand, to guard our minds against disquiet when the good is long delayed.

The beautiful virtue of hope is allied to longanimity; we almost always discover it to be the basis of the latter virtue. Hope, on the one hand, bids us to have confidence in God, reminding us that He will not deny us strength, however protracted our endeavor may be. On the other hand, hope makes it easier to understand the importance of prolonged activity; it makes it possible for us to draw quietly on the reserves of prudence, which teaches us how to wait, so that we may act at the right time. *Festina lente* ("make haste slowly"): this will be the result of the cooperation between the various virtues.

Longanimity conforms us to the inner laws of work

Almost every sort of work consists of a series of acts, of tiny acts performed in succession, which together build up a new good. There must exist a certain plan in this process, to unite the separate acts; there must also be the inevitable pause between one act and another, and between different groups of acts. All of this creates the whole technique of work, with its own strict and binding rules. And it is the virtue of longanimity that brings our will into conformity with the laws and techniques of work.

There are a great many types of work that are so subject to their own laws of action that one cannot interfere with them without injury to the good that is their goal. To incline our will to respect for these laws, we summon longanimity to our aid.

Longanimity is particularly necessary in educational and directive work. For whenever it is a question of influencing other people, it is necessary to let some time go by, so that the sown seed may take root and yield its fruit. Violent activity is like rain that flows away when it falls on parched ground; the earth is not able to absorb all the good of which it had such need. A young man, loaded with important and valuable advice, is not able to take it all in immediately or to draw all the benefit from it that he might. One must take into account his capacity for absorption. It is just the same with the whole process of teaching, which must always be spread out over many years, even though its duration causes boredom in the young.

In every sort of interior spiritual work, which holds a promise of peace and happiness for us only in the kingdom of Heaven, we must make up our minds to engage in prolonged effort. The uprooting of bad habits and the practice of virtues proceed slowly and demand long activity.

In almost every type of external daily work, longanimity plays a big part. For these works have their own laws, which should be respected. Many types of work need to be performed slowly, carefully, and meticulously. Let us look at factory work, where one simple action is repeated in the same way several times every minute; or at laboratory work, in which it takes a thousand, maybe two thousand, similar experiments to establish one fragmentary truth. The great inventors, the benefactors of mankind who arrived at their discoveries by wearisome, boring labor, excelled in the virtue of longanimity.

Every kind of art comes into being only with the help of longanimity. At its first inception some sort of technical skill is latent, which must be perfected by a long series of studies and exercises. The musician, before he becomes a virtuoso, must endure the unpleasant sound of boring scales, which torture his creative aspirations and tear at the nerves of those around him. The painter or sculptor wastes a lot of paper on sketches before his eye develops sureness of line in drawing and sensitivity in coloring. We marvel at the embroidery on the vestments preserved in the cathedrals of Plock or Wawel. What slow, wearisome work, sometimes the work of a whole lifetime, was concentrated on a little piece of material!

We come into contact with the great services of the virtue of longanimity at every step of our daily life. Let us look at the work of the gardener grafting trees whose fruit he will never taste. Let us remind ourselves of the words spoken by the apostle James concerning the toil of the farmer: "Be patient therefore, brethren, until the coming of the Lord. Behold the husbandman waits for the precious fruit of the earth: patiently waiting until he receives the early and later rain. Therefore you must also be patient, and strengthen your hearts."[129]

Nature develops unusual patience and longanimity in us. The seed thrown into the earth, surrendered to cold, snows, and frost, will seem useless lying in the mud, but it is a sign of a certain hope, of trust in the earth, that this loving mother will not waste it but will yield fruit a hundredfold in "the appointed time."[130]

Longanimity teaches us to work effectively

The virtue of longanimity has its own pedagogy, since its task is to train something in us.

We are reminded of the strange episode in the book of Judges, when Gideon set forth against the Midianites. An assembly of warriors gathered together, ready for the battle, but the Lord considered that there were too many of them and that Israel might overestimate its share in the victory. An appeal to the frightened and cowardly that they should return home diminished the ranks. But still too many remained, so a new test followed. God commanded Gideon to lead the army to water. Then whoever drank from the stream direct with his mouth would not be eligible for the battle, while those who scooped up the water with their hands would be retained. Three hundred were left, and with them, through Gideon, God conquered. The only people that God considered fit for the battle were those who were able to take up the water handful after handful to their mouths and thus quench their thirst — in other words, men who were not hasty.[131] This is God's pedagogy.

[129] James 5:7-8.

[130] Ps. 144:15 (RSV = Ps. 145:15).

[131] Judg. 7:1-9.

In almost every type of work there is room for such an approach — not haste, which hurls us into work without reflection, but deliberation, tranquillity, and prudence, which bid us, in all our work, to remember not only its beginning but its end. In sum, we need an intelligent, balanced distribution of strength. We must not waste it by the crazy speed with which we start work; we have to conserve it to the end.

It is not enough to know with what strength we undertake our work; we also need to ask ourselves how much we shall have left when we come to finish it. The labor that brings our work to its conclusion is twice as hard when we have set about it unwisely, for in addition to the ordinary exhausting efforts, there is the extra labor that comes of our inability to distribute our efforts properly. The work that is undertaken and completed with a wise distribution of energy has virtue and longanimity in it. *Festina lente*, "make haste slowly."

The pedagogy of longanimity is also expressed in the fact that it teaches us humility in our desires. "Not my will but Thine be done."[132] The human will carries us away, but God's will encourages us to moderation. God's will fixes human work in a framework of physical and spiritual laws. We need to act cautiously, carefully, and sensibly; we need to distribute our powers, for the best human material is sometimes wasted by lack of restraint in one's work. It lacks sufficient profundity or thoroughness.

Long-suffering teaches us respect for God's laws as expressed in the techniques of work and in the properties of nature. If some work is hard, this is not merely the result of Original Sin; it also comes from resistance to the order that God established in the created world. Nature does not admit of gaps in the established order. God's longanimity is expressed in nature's activity, which we

[132] Luke 22:42.

admire in the evolutionary process of becoming, growing, and coming to maturity.

Let us take a closer look at the slow growth of corn. Human impatience would like to speed it up with artificial light and heat so that in one season it might yield a double, even triple harvest. But meanwhile the unhurried action of God gives time and energy to the development of the roots and the formation of the ear. We ask what all this is for. And yet does not the whole strength of the plant, enabling it to withstand great storms, come from this fact?

In the slow development and ripening of fruit, in the growth of a baby, and in the seasons of the year, we can see the divine scheme of things: longanimity, which leaves time for the consolidation of all that has been achieved.

Longanimity keeps us from hasty, shoddy work

The governing force in the work of contemporary man is sometimes an itch to possess. We give way to a rebellious impatience that wants everything we see, in large quantities and very quickly. Here is where revolution begins. It wants to achieve great things, many things, gigantic things. It wants, at times, to do violence to the nature of creation. History teaches, however, that it is not so much revolution as peaceful, evolutionary human work that brings us forward on the path of lasting progress. Unfortunately, man too often believes in the power of revolution and so destroys his own strength prematurely. He gives way to the fever of creating. He wants to achieve in the shortest possible time something that can only be of all-around benefit when it is accomplished within the fixed natural laws of human activity.

Examples from physical or technical work can illustrate certain dangerous illusions. For the sake of temporary successes people are snatched away from the full range of their daily tasks and prodded into feverish work that is only productive at the cost of the spiritual life. Man is torn away from the fullness of his destiny. Sometimes the only people who are well regarded are those who have stifled all their other inclinations, sacrificing them on the altar of productive work. Such people are imbued with new ideas of social usefulness, which they equate with the highest output of physical work. It is easy to give in to these illusions, particularly when one observes that in every field of human life it is possible to get everything done by violence and force. We would even like to force God into compliance with our will.

Instead of the words "If You wish it, I can certainly do so," we say, "I want it; therefore You must do it!" Our "philosophy of action" does not usually take the laws of God's grace into account; and yet God will give us the fruit of our work "at the appointed time." Every grace comes in its own good time, which has been settled by God. We must have the humility of long-suffering, confident that God will not leave us without His help.

With the lack of long-suffering is connected another phenomenon of the present time: the low quality of our feverish work. We see it in architecture, painting, sculpture, and the production of industry. These are not the manifestations of virtues; one might more truly say that they show all the vices: impatience and a lack of conscientiousness and perseverance. Human desires and lusts peep out from these new works, which will not stand up to the passage of time. The works of the ancients have not succumbed to the ravages of time, but there are many monuments of our own age that will not remain after a few decades even as respectable ruins.

Rubbish is covering and besmirching the world. A great deal is being produced, but it is valueless. The notion that quantity can take the place of quality is illusory. Statistics kill us; the spell of numbers wearies and demoralizes us. We always ask, "How much?" and we scarcely ever ask, "How good is it?"

Here is the origin of the aimless overproduction, which by no means satisfies the needs of all the hungry and naked people in the world, and of the irrational exploitation of goods that ought to be preserved for future generations. The way to conquer this sickness is to put the question "How good is it?" in place of the question "How much?" In other words, we must put quality above temporary achievements of quantity.

This will occur with the help of longanimity, long-suffering, and forbearance, when that virtue appears in the noble company of charity, joy, peace, patience, and goodness. We must learn this Gideonite virtue, that we may drink from a hard-working life, handful by handful.

16

Perseverance and Constancy in Work

In undertaking any sort of work we must keep in mind the warning that "that man will be saved who endures to the last."[133]

In every type of work the goal is most important, for every activity has some object. The goal attracts the will and inclines it to perseverance and constancy in its efforts.

Perseverance is persistence toward a chosen goal

What is perseverance? It is a prudent, constant, and continual persistence in a rationally taken decision to strive toward some desired good. The decision we take must be prudent and rational, because by it we are assessing both our goal and the means leading to its achievement. A rational, thought-out decision will thenceforth enlighten all our efforts, in spite of increasing difficulties. When emotion leads us astray, the will is always stimulated to endurance by a prudently taken decision.

[133]Matt. 24:13.

Perseverance is a distinct virtue; as such, it will encourage us to practice the virtues and works shown to us by reason, whatever obstacles may ensue from the prolonged nature of our activity.

When in our daily work, we confront the difficulties of protracted effort, we shall be led to develop in ourselves virtues of which, perhaps, we had never before felt the need. Each of the other virtues is concerned with itself alone and is a virtue insofar as it perseveres to the end. Chastity, fortitude, humility, and goodness are revealed only in the final act. On the other hand, perseverance derives its tenacity from the very nobility that exists in carrying a job through to the end, despite the weariness that comes from the long continuance of our labors. The inner obligation arising from our decision to work, our undertaking of work, is our very conscience: we must not turn aside from this work. We feel there is something wrong in abandoning any work we have undertaken, even when there are no witnesses to our infidelity.

Perseverance can be interpreted in three ways: as a state of mind in which we steadfastly resist sadness, as a decision to "stick it out," and as the actual carrying through of our work to the end. Perseverance therefore expresses not only a state of mind but also a state of will.

From these explanations may be seen the real, distinctive object of the virtue of perseverance: hard-working activity, whose very protractedness can lead to sadness. And so we stand on the borderline of the two virtues of longanimity and perseverance.

Almost every type of activity and work has its highest point of tension, its peak of hardship, which we fear. It is significant that even work that is undertaken with joy, that we like and find pleasant, has this turning point, before which we feel a certain fear. On this point it very often depends whether or not our effort holds out to the end. Here certainly is God's mystery of work, in which every action has its share of salutary toil.

It is in light of situations like this that the virtue of perseverance performs its task: it has to control the effects produced in us by protracted work.

Constancy is fidelity to plans and intentions

The virtue of constancy *(constantia)* makes us capable of striving after the good we have in mind, whatever obstacles may arise from external causes. The scope of its task is therefore wider. While perseverance specializes in helping us through heavy work, this virtue of constancy embraces in one wide sweep all the difficulties that may come up in the course of our work. It instills in us faithfulness to our plans and intentions — in spite of everything, no matter what may happen. The difficulties are not hidden from us; we do not know whether they will be temporary or protracted, slight and nagging or violent and sudden, and it is all the same to us. Armed with constancy, we calmly await even the most unpleasant surprises.

Perseverance and constancy are closely related

What relation is there between perseverance and constancy, and between these two and the other virtues?

The kinship of perseverance with constancy lies in the fact that both these virtues are distinguished by a strong persistence in some good toward which they tend. They both coincide in their aim; they differ in the sort of difficulty they have to overcome. In the case of perseverance, it is the difficulties arising from protracted activity; in the case of constancy, it is every other kind of difficulty.

In the acquisition of the other virtues, perseverance will be more important than constancy, for perseverance goes more to the inner essence of every virtue. Every virtue that we mean to acquire demands persevering activity. Therefore the vital factor in the acquisition of every virtue is perseverance in our progress toward it, because it revolves around the difficulties caused by continued activity over a long period of time.

Constancy has a closer connection with perseverance than with patience. Constancy and perseverance are united in their aim, which is the good intended; and they join forces with patience to overcome the obstacles on the way to that good.

Daily work requires both perseverance and constancy

We must now consider the ascetic basis of perseverance and constancy, virtues that are so useful for daily work. The first book of Kings exhorts us: "Serve the Lord with all your heart. And turn not aside after vain things which shall never profit you nor deliver you, because they are vain."[134]

A very important warning! Before any work, we have to make the decision to push on to the goal pointed out to us by reason.

The first thing is the proper acceptance of the appointed task: in other words, joy at the thought of the good we expect from our work. As a matter of fact, real sadness is an exceptional thing at the start. If, indeed, protest rises up in us from the very beginning, we should examine our conscience, the motives for our opposition, and the rightness of our intentions. But since our tendency to good is natural, while the tendency to evil is not, we usually begin any new undertaking in the right disposition. The sadness usually comes later when the difficulties of the work mount up: then we start giving in to our changing moods and want to shake off our oppressive duty. Now our sense of duty is put to the test.

[134] 1 Kings 12:20-21 (RSV = 1 Sam. 12:20-21).

Temptations arise: the longing for new work, unfaithfulness in the work we have already undertaken or that has been entrusted to us, the desire for a change of occupation and this, sometimes, for some quite trivial reason. There is always a certain streak of betrayal in these feelings.

Here in Poland, this is one of our national faults and can be seen in our daily work. Our mentality is somewhat volatile, sensitive to everything, always ready to accept something new and to cast aside what is familiar and has stood the test of time. It is strange: with all our wealth of initiative, we lack the will for completion, for carrying things through to the end. Our national life in this spiritual cross-section looks like a great field, on which stand a number of unfinished buildings. Readiness for work, facility, and the first glow of enthusiasm deserted us halfway through our project; they did not stand up to the first difficulties, and perseverance and constancy were not there to overcome them.

How close to all men at times is the emotion of Ecclesiastes: "And again I hated all my application wherewith I had earnestly labored under the sun. . . . Wherefore I left off and my heart renounced laboring any more under the sun. . . . For what profit shall a man have of all his labor and vexation of spirit, with which he hath been tormented under the sun?"[135]

The good aim, the thoughtfully reached decision, and the intended good: all are forgotten and tend rather to increase our anguish of soul.

We have then to call on the values arising from the two virtues in question, perseverance and constancy. They keep us on the path of fidelity and uprightness both in relation to ourselves and to the people who trust us.

[135]Eccles. 2:18, 20, 22.

17

Conscientiousness and Diligence

St. Paul warned the faithful in Colossae to retain in their work the connection with God, toward whom all activity should be directed: "Give your human masters full obedience, not with that show of service that tries to win human favor, but single-mindedly, in fear of the Lord. Work at all your tasks with a will, reminding yourselves that you do it for the Lord, not for men; and you may be assured that the Lord will give the portion He has allotted you in return."[136]

Most people are usually ready and willing for every sort of work; what they lack is the ability to bring it to a successful conclusion. The Apostle knew the mystery of human work, for he warned the Corinthians: "It remains for you to complete your action; readiness of will must be completed by deeds as far as your means allow. We value a man's readiness of will according to the means he has, not according to the means he might have, but has not."[137]

[136]Col. 3:22-24.
[137]2 Cor. 8:11-12.

It is only the ready will to see the task through, not the mere initial desire to work, that produces any results. Unfortunately the willingness to desire is usually greater than the willingness to act. We all know the causes that gradually weaken the willingness to act; they lead to carelessness, unreliability, lack of perseverance, and the tendency to abandon half-completed tasks.

Conscientiousness is necessary in work

Almost everyone, when he undertakes some new task, intends to perform it well, conscientiously, and nobly. For the human will, even when it is weak, naturally tends to want to carry out well whatever it has taken on.

Where then is the borderline, the limit of conscientiousness? Is there not a shortage of really conscientious workers who are dissatisfied with their own best efforts?

There is endless anxiety about whether we have brought the object of the work to the highest measure of perfection. The "golden mean" is wanting, even in the will to do what is right.

How does one gauge, therefore, the full measure of conscientiousness, that point at which one can be certain that one need add nothing more to one's actions?

Conscientious work fulfils four conditions

In order to make certain that human work achieves the highest level accessible to man, four conditions are necessary. The work must be done in accordance with its own goal, in accordance with the nature of its object, in the proper order, and in accordance with the perfection that the object of the work should have.

Work acquires its value and is conscientious when it is in accordance with its own goal. We say about badly done work that "it should have been done differently." This "should have been done" relates to the goal of the work, to what was supposed to have been achieved. The consciousness of the goal and the will toward it are the origin of the perfection of action and, at the same time, its final stage of completion.

Secondly, to reach its highest level, work must be done in accordance with the nature of its object. This varies, a fact that we must take into consideration right from the start. In our conscientiousness, we must not overstep the measure of our actual object, or we shall undo it. The addition of new material perfections must never go beyond what is fitting to the nature of the object.

Thirdly, conscientious work is performed in its own proper order. The word *order* holds for us associations with the idea of a *sequence*. In every sequence there is some harmony, evaluation, human thought, and judgment. Conscientious work is systematic, judicious, planned, and prudent. Now, to retain this order during the progress of the work, we must keep the work as a whole steadily in mind, to establish its starting point, its course, and its point of completion. This demands calm, patience, and real planning, so as not to waste time on superfluous considerations. With the aid of reflection we notice the constituent parts of the work we have undertaken, and the alternation of activity. Different temptations can spring from lack of reflection: the temptation to start in the middle, at the end, or with the easier and more pleasant tasks. This usually leads to confusion, which makes work more difficult or frustrates it completely.

Finally, to achieve the proper measure of conscientiousness, we must act in accordance with the proper perfection that the object of the work ought to possess. For everything has its own perfection, which is the pinnacle of what is attainable by it.

In what does the proper perfection of a given work, its proper virtue, consist? This is a hard and much debated problem. There is no lack of people who spend their whole lives improving their works. There are artists who repaint their pictures, writers who tear up their manuscripts time after time, sculptors who smash their own works of art. In our own work we also see a thousand faults, magnified sometimes by indecision or just by plain pride.

Here, therefore, we should learn to find the real golden mean, beyond which there is no need to go. For often the *better* is the enemy of the *good*. St. John Bosco used to say that he preferred "this good today rather than that better thing tomorrow." We all know of many good things that never came into being merely because everyone was waiting for something better. There have been talented people who have not left anything behind them, even though they had the duty and the possibility of doing so.

I think that we get to the heart of a matter when we differentiate the external perfection of an act from its internal perfection. The external perfection of an act usually has its limits; this is because well-directed diligence and conscientiousness are linked with the usual laws of physical and moral activity to which we are subject. The material objects we use in our work or to which it is related, have a limited and finite character; it is possible to give them a strictly finite perfection to which nothing more could be added even if we spent years of further effort and ingenuity on them. Michelangelo could improve some details in his masterpiece but, in the final analysis, his *Pietà* is a completed work of art. And where the ordinary products of work are concerned, the possibilities are still less. Matter sets limits to further possibilities.

On the other hand, when it comes to the inner value of work, there are usually no limits to the perfection attainable. We can say of a man who lives according to God's grace and the Christian virtues that are his duty, that he is holy and that his work is perfect. Nevertheless, to the extent that his love for God increases and the intentions of his work become purer, new perfections are added to those he already has. In this sort of work, one can always go one step further, for there can always be greater love for God and greater giving of oneself to God in work. The whole spiritual worth of a man can have a great effect on the value of human work; it can raise it up continually.

Therefore we must transfer the problem of perfection in external work to the supernatural sphere, instead of improving purely external values *ad infinitum*. Thanks to this, spiritual progress is always possible by means of external work. Having reached the limits of perfection in our daily work, we transfer the *raison d'être* of our goals to our inner state, and find a horizon of infinity and eternity opening out to us.

This gives people who work for love of God their superiority over those who do not have this motive. The latter aim at purely external perfection, whereas the former can always transfer their efforts to that inner perfecting, which can go on indefinitely.

Conscientiousness and diligence

With conscientiousness goes diligence, which is the zealous performance of one's duties. It arms us against the tendency to dawdle over our work, or to postpone it without a proper reason. Diligence is also closely allied to long-suffering. The former stimulates to activity, the latter moderates; and this has a good effect on the work being done. Diligence performs this brotherly service for long-suffering by rousing it from any stagnation that might occur. These are the things that oppose diligence: delay through laziness, a dawdling attitude to work, failure to do it by the promised time, giving in to discouragement and dejection, and everything that makes our work drag on endlessly.

Diligence is supported by punctuality, the daughter of order and harmony, whose rule is to do everything at the right time and according to a definite plan. Closely allied to diligence are integrity and reliability, the outward sign and the fruit of diligent work.

Then we reach the stage of attaching such value to our promise that to say "I promise" is as good as saying "It's done." Knowing the value of our word, we are careful in making promises and undertaking obligations. This is a very beautiful virtue, and one that wards off many illusions. Indeed, it is greatly needed by all those people of "good will" who bind themselves before they have fully understood what is involved and without thinking at all of the importance of keeping their word.

Fidelity to one's promises will result from the proper appreciation of what it is to give one's word seriously.

Conscientious work reveals the worth of the worker

The inner worth of a man is revealed to a large extent in his conscientious work.

It is difficult to arrive at any external estimate of conscientiousness; we have to look for an inner measure of it. This principle comes into conflict with the contemporary organization of work, which uses wholly external tests for the maintenance and development of conscientiousness. It says, "The problem of conscientiousness and obedience is the problem of control." If the work is performed in the time determined beforehand, the worker is held to be conscientious. With the abandonment of internal criteria, more trust is put in clocks, foremen, and in the management and organization of work than in the inner standard of morality and in the worker's conscience.

Man's conscience is left "hanging on the wall" instead of acting within him. Such simplification, important for external order and for productive planning, is demoralizing, because the test of conscience is in feet and yards rather than in terms of actual human possibilities. The worker has a clock in front of him and declares, "I have lots of time; I needn't hurry." If he has lots of time, he wastes lots of it.

Is there not a conflict between the attempt to educate people through work and the fact that work is given over almost exclusively to external control?

A technical evaluation of human work is not enough. For it is not the man who has done his job within the time laid down by a meter who is conscientious, but rather the one who has done it conscientiously within the time that is appropriate to the particular task and his own capabilities.

Conscience is the true judge of conscientiousness

Technology is a lifeless force; it cannot, therefore, estimate the value of the activity of a rational and free being. The subjection of human work to technical tests only degrades man and renders him totally material. We must also be guided by that internal measure that is the conscience of man. Technical evaluation is only an additional means; it is not the measure of human morality and conscientiousness. For it may happen that a man who has performed a job in the given time is still not conscientious, for he may have been capable of doing it in less time, or perhaps should have taken longer over it.

A man must take into account the external conditions of his work, but he may not ignore his own capabilities; the just evaluation is the *moral* evaluation, and the measure of it must be the conscience by which man is responsible before God.

The measure of Catholic conscientiousness in work is found in these words of St. Paul: "Give your human masters full obedience, not with that show of service which tries to win human favor, but single-mindedly, in fear of the Lord. Work at all your tasks with a will, reminding yourselves that you are doing it for the Lord, not for men; and you may be sure that the Lord will give you the portion He has allotted you in return."[138]

The external criterion is not the test of our conscientiousness. God is its measure, "with a good will serving, as to the Lord, and not to men."[139] "And each man's workmanship will be plainly seen. It is the day of the Lord that will disclose it, since that day is to reveal itself in fire, and fire will test the quality of each man's workmanship."[140]

Here is the measure of Christian conscientiousness! The book of Proverbs instructs us about it: "If thou say, 'I have not strength enough,' He that seeth into the heart, He understandeth; nothing deceiveth the keeper of thy soul, and He shall render to a man according to his works."[141] The measure of conscientiousness is the heart, into which God is continually looking.

The value of such a measure of activity is a hundred times higher, for from it flow courage and efficiency, an ever better intention and an ever deeper faithfulness to God. On it is based ever greater perfection, which is restricted so far as material limits go, but which is infinite as regards interior work. It leads us from the perfection of daily work to eternal perfection.

[138]Col. 3:22-24.

[139]Eph. 6:7.

[140]1 Cor. 3:13.

[141]Prov. 24:12.

18

Silence in Work

The result of all human work should be not merely the perfecting of the thing produced, but also the perfecting of the worker; not merely external order in work, but also inner order in man.

All work creates order

The passage in Genesis that shows how God produces the world from chaos stands as a model of the universal ordering: "In the beginning God created Heaven and earth. And the earth was void and empty, and darkness was upon the face of the deep; and the Spirit of God moved over the waters."[142] This void, emptiness, and darkness must have been horrible. The one consolation and hope was the Spirit of God.

But here is God's command: "Let there be light!"[143] God sets about creating order. The light wins God's approval. The Creator

[142]Gen. 1:1-2.
[143]Gen. 1:3.

has separated the light from the darkness, and a new order arises. In these beautiful, concise, and extremely simple images in Genesis we perceive the stages of the divine ordering. It is an object lesson for the working man.

At the start of almost every type of work we meet with chaos and disorder. The image of the task before us is shapeless and without dimensions. In addition, it is hard to see where we must start. There is still uncertainty in our mind as to the choice of the means of action; we cannot see clearly what we are aiming at. All we know is that as a result of our activity, a certain order has to arise. For the greatest and most general goal of working life is the production of order.

However, the actual process of getting down to the work, in its initial phases, usually increases the disorder and chaos, both in our own minds and in what we are doing. Sometimes for weeks there is nothing to hint at the order that is to be brought forth.

Let us stand at the entrance of a factory. Within its order, disturbance and racket resound. In all this uproar, man is a completely strange phenomenon. He is overwhelmed by the infernal clatter and disorder.

Let us look at him through the eyes of the poet Wojciech Bak:

And you? See what they have made of you now.
You, idolater of the age of this choking nightmare
They have counted you, measured you, marked you out,
With an ax cut you off from the land.
With the hysterical whistle, the groan of the sirens
As with a scourge they have torn your heart to pieces.
From machine gone mad in a vortex
You come as a robot — deafened and dumb,
And the man has gone! No more than a body,
A corpse seized by the rush of a turbine.

The man has gone — left in the turmoil
Are only lifeless active machines.[144]

But there is no need to look for factories. The whole world is rapidly becoming more and more one great factory. The streets of a city draw man into a vortex no less than the factory's snake pit of conveyer belts. Within the city's order there is a sort of disorder, a lack of harmony that attracts but fatigues.

In addition there is the fever, the bustle of every day, of almost every hour. When we stand on the threshold of a new day, confronted by the daily program in all its detail, at that moment we know uneasiness and fear.

This whole problem is growing more obtrusive today. Let us consider it in relation to the question of quiet and peace in work.

Silence is a condition for fruitful work

And here "in the beginning" — as in all of God's works — the rational will should have its say. "Let there be light"; let darkness be scattered, that we may see what actually has to be done. Without light one cannot see what one's task is. In the midst of the initial chaos and turmoil, one has to enter into oneself, to become calm, and to form and foster quiet in oneself. Why must one do this? Because silence and quietness are the essential conditions for fruitfulness in every type of work, whether we are dealing with supernatural action, the world of science, or just ordinary daily work.

Who does not know descriptions of the quiet of the convent or the hermit's cell? We know it from novels, treatises, the *Conferences* of Cassian, and from the life of Benedictines, Trappists, and

[144]Wojciech Bak, "Idolaters of the Twentieth Century."

Carthusians. We are filled with jealousy and longing for this quiet. We see in it the mystery of sanctification and a safe path to Heaven. In Benedictine monasteries quiet was so highly valued that the monks were urged, while engaged in physical work, to listen to the reading that went on when a group of them were working together.

The quiet of the interior life has its beautiful model in the house of Nazareth and in the quiet of the upper room at Pentecost when the Apostles were waiting for the Paraclete. The Church grew and became powerful in the great quiet of the catacombs where, by torchlight, the martyrs, the first Christians, humbled themselves before God.

Every great work and every great sanctification is born in silence and recollection. The more deeply people develop their interior life, the more they are won over to silence. When the saints start to speak less and less, when they fall deeply in love with silence, they listen ever more intently to what the Spirit of God says to the Church. They become "slow to speak."[145] Man listens intently to God's silence, to God's voice, which speaks to him in that silence.

It is just the same in the world of learning. People who want to carry out something look for seclusion; they impose silence on themselves until "the harvest time." The scholar who is full of talk, always in high spirits, who is too smooth and sociable, does not arouse confidence. The use of thought and the need for silence both in speech and writing demand concentration, the shutting of oneself up within oneself.

But even in external physical work there is a sort of mysterious longing for quiet. This may be noticed particularly in work that is full of strain and effort. Such work always longs for quiet.

[145]James 1:19.

Silence in Work

We have often felt the beauty of labor in the fields. Polish painters are in love with this motif. They show on the far horizon a horse, with heavily drooping head, dragging the plow as it turns the soil; and after it a man, bent with toil, staring into the open furrow and treading in slow concentration, step after step. What an almost tangible silence there is in this scene! It contains only two figures. The mystery of piercing into the bosom of the earth takes place in silence. The plowman is usually a silent man. So also is the sower. The seed sown by him falls in all quietness, without a sound. . . .

And the miner? Miners are the most silent people of all. Their heavy work in the darkness under the earth so affects them that even in the sunlight up on the surface they still do not emerge from their silence.

The contemporary development of daily work, although it takes place in the midst of tumult and disorder, forces people increasingly to isolation of thought, concentration, and the straining of their attention. The driver of an express train, the pilot, and the chauffeur: each must acquire concentration and self-control; each must rid himself of all superfluous sensations, and recollect himself in his silence.

In the technique of contemporary work it is becoming increasingly clear that wherever circumstances demand an increased exertion of one's powers, this immediately leads to silence, as if it were a rule that fruitful work and lack of attention were incompatible. Every strain in work closes our lips and, at times, our eyes to everything that is superfluous. We stand at the edge of the interior asceticism of work. The efficiency of every task depends on one's freedom from superfluous dissipation of effort and on the curtailing of unnecessary movements. By training ourselves in this way, we arrive at the ability to exercise control over ourselves, to concentrate and to be quiet.

And because of the importance of the problem of quiet in work, we are right to inquire about the way to achieve it.

We should seek inner quiet even amid hectic work

"The great silence" ought to be accomplished not only around us but, above all, within us.[146] Tired of the chaos and hubbub of work, people long for quiet, and most often look for it around themselves.

But quiet is born, not so much around us, as within ourselves. To be quiet and concentrated does not mean that one has to be in a peaceful, cloisterlike, deserted place, far from all tumult. To say this would be an oversimplification, and would not solve the problem at all.

To be quiet means to have quiet in one's soul. And this is something completely different. It is possible to be quiet and have quietness in one's soul in the middle of the rowdiest street, of the noisiest work, or of the most earsplitting din of the factory. We must acquire our own quiet. Of course, one can do something to lessen the tumult of external life, and this is a very necessary thing. One can also guard against the creation of unnecessary noise; but none of this will solve the real problem unless we have quiet within ourselves.

In our search for quiet we must, naturally, summon isolation and solitude to our aid. But we should not overestimate them, particularly in the arrangement of social life today. For it is an almost impossible thing to achieve solitude in daily work. Nor is solitude necessary to achieve silence. Isolation does not constitute

[146]"The great silence" refers to the monastic custom (prescribed in chapter 42 of *The Rule of St. Benedict*) of maintaining absolute silence during the night after the recitation of Compline, the final office of the day.

the perfection of our life. It can be a helpful condition of it, and an appropriate instrument of the interior life.

Yet, one can be isolated and not alone. Indeed, at times a man with all the proper conditions for isolation has all of Hell inside him. Complete solitude in daily work would be something abnormal. For man must join in his work with God and with his neighbors.

Perfect solitude in work will depend not on leaving the world, but on remaining in the presence of God. It is not this occupation or that, this type of work or that, but only our inner relation to God that confirms our solitude and quiet. Only then are we continually alone with God.

This is so because God fills the whole world. In every detail of our work we come across the traces of God's hand: in things and in people, in our environment and in the powers that we use. We are unceasingly plunged in God, "for in Him we live and move and have our being."[147]

To be solitary means to share in God's solitude. We must learn to acquire this art in our daily work as an indispensable condition of our quiet. The direction of oneself toward God and toward solitude in Him prepare the soul for the acquisition of that peace that helps us in the most distracting, most active external work. In this sense, man can retain his solitude and quiet even in the uproar of factory work, in the middle of the street, or during the labor of the harvest. He attains a state of entering into himself, of concentrating, which this hush within oneself always accompanies.

Certainly, the silence of the lips, within the limits shown by reason, also has its task. Man's silence makes room for God's word. When man is silent, God is heard. And once we listen intently to God we maintain our silence even in the midst of our speech.

[147] Acts 17:28.

Virtues help us to acquire inner quiet in work

"Everything around man makes far less noise than man himself. The echo that magnifies external things in our soul — this is the real uproar." This is a penetrating truth. We often do an injustice to the external world in blaming it for forcing us into distraction and noise. The longings of our soul, the disorder of our ideas and our thoughts, the diversity of our aims: it is these things that make the tumult inside us. Only our inner spiritual attitude can seal the entrance through which all these stray scraps tumble into our soul. If it is possible to open this door, it is also possible to close it.

"A voice crying in the wilderness" has to announce to the soul, "Make straight the way of the Lord."[148]

In order to practice quiet within oneself, it is necessary to call on the aid of the virtues: patience, which calms the torment of sadness in us; perseverance and constancy, which overcome disquiet and fickleness, the shifting of intentions, plans, and goals from one object to another. Longanimity (or long-suffering) plays its part by controlling the feverish disturbance of work; humility and disinterestedness conquer the desire we feel for attention. Through the latter, our work takes on the subtle quality of a deed maturing in secret, like a flower in the bud until the time comes for it to bloom. The longing for renown, the proclamation of our own deeds and sometimes even only of our plans, rob us of peace and of real thoroughness in our work, for there is too much for display in them, too much that is done for applause and renown, and too much seeking for immediate payment "before sunset."

The spirit of quiet demands humility and disinterestedness; the spirit of calm, as the fruit of love and justice, brings with it order and concord, and drives out disputes, discord, quarrelsomeness,

[148]Isa. 40:3; Mark 1:3.

and division. All of these are the fruit of quiet, poured into the soul of the working man.

In comparison, mere quiet in our surroundings has less meaning. It is, of course, necessary to get rid of unnecessary noise and disorder in work; but when man does not possess quiet within himself, the quiet of his surroundings does not help much.

The love of one's neighbor, however, demands that we should not make the work of others difficult by our mode of behavior. In quiet work there arises, at times, the temptation that His accusers proposed to Christ: "This is no place for thee; go to Judea, so that thy disciples also may see thy doings. Nobody is content to act in secret, if he wishes to make himself known at large; if thou must needs act thus, show thyself before the world."[149]

This temptation is continually penetrating man's defenses: "This is too small a field of action. I am made for greater things!" But Christ had an answer ready: "My time has not come yet."[150] This had to satisfy them. And this has to suffice for us until the time comes when quiet, hidden work has developed new values in us: "My good and faithful servant; since thou hast been faithful over little things, I have great things to commit to thy charge."[151]

Then every advance we make will be a confirmation of our actual abilities in work. We shall be protected against illusions and shall not be the cause of disappointment.

[149] John 7:3-4.
[150] John 7:6.
[151] Matt. 25:23.

19

Cooperation

Human work has its own needs, above all of which are direction and division of work.

Direction is necessary because in the course of work there must be someone who is aware of the broad thought behind it and its general aim, who understands the work in its entirety and watches over its correct course. At the head of every enterprise there must stand the "architect" in whose hands all the threads come together and who is the center of the whole scheme. Yet wherever there is authority or direction there must also be subordinates ready to act according to the superior's ideas.

The second necessity of human work is division of labor. Every job needs to be split into individual small tasks, which must then be entrusted to different people who act either simultaneously or alternately.

Out of both these needs cooperation is born. The direction and division of work give rise to numerous different relationships between co-workers. It is not always easy to give expression to them or to put a name on them, for at times they are elusive because they penetrate into the depths of the soul and there mold the attitudes of co-workers toward each other.

These hidden, inaccessible feelings affect the course of work for good, or else check it, or even make it frankly impossible. The whole interior life of work is contained in them. Now this relationship depends on the social attitudes in work, on the personal values of the directors and subordinates, and on the natural and supernatural resources at the disposal of the co-workers. This relationship is influenced by personal virtues, both by general virtues and by those special ones that are particularly connected with work. Our interior relation to work will depend on what we have at our disposal not only by way of instruments of work, but also in terms of moral and spiritual values.

The spirit of cooperation is essential in work

The divine Wisdom laid down what the spiritual relationships between people should be in these words: "Bear each other's burdens; and so you will fulfil Christ's law."[152]

Every law, every order, every command given to us, and every action we undertake, must develop in the spirit of cooperation.

Both superiors and subordinates have their own burdens in work. They must help each other to bear them and to fulfil their individual tasks. A wise saying expresses this picturesquely: "The bird carries the wings and the wings carry the bird." Mutual aid is necessary. And so it is with the interrelations of those who give orders and those who receive them. The spirit of cooperation and service must illumine them.

Christ showed us beautifully what should constitute the spirit of cooperation between superior and subordinates. There is, for

[152]Gal. 6:2.

example, an incident with the sons of Zebedee. Their mother made a strange request: "Here are my sons; grant that in Thy kingdom one may take his place on Thy right and the other on Thy left."[153] Jesus was not annoyed by the spirit of this request, but explained to His disciples the new way of living together that should obtain among people in a Christian society: "You know that among the Gentiles, those who bear rule lord it over them, and great men vaunt their power over them. This is the old order, but it must pass away. With you it must be otherwise; whoever would be a great man among you, must be your servant, and whoever has a mind to be first among you, must be your slave. So it is that the Son of Man did not come to have service done Him; He came to serve others, and to give His life as a ransom for the lives of many."[154]

And the second striking incident occurs at the Last Supper. Christ, at the feet of His disciples, said, "Do you understand what it is I have done to you?" They did not understand. "Why then, if I have washed your feet, I who am the Master and the Lord, you in your turn ought to wash each other's feet; I have been setting you an example, which will teach you in your turn to do what I have done for you."[155]

This is the image of the new relationship between superiors and subordinates. A bishop kissing the feet of a poor man in the *Mandatum* of Holy Thursday: this signifies the spirit of service on the part of superiors in the Christian life.

In an old manuscript in the Vatican library one finds a significant illumination representing the Pope — the servant of the servants of God — as a footstool supporting a bishop who is

[153]Matt. 20:21.

[154]Matt. 20:25-28.

[155]John 13:12, 14-15.

fighting a dragon. This is how the *Pontifex Maximus* appears in the spirit of the Church.

Nor can it be otherwise in the field of Catholic politics. *To rule* must be synonymous with *to serve*. For all Christian authority the same is true.

In work this ideal of service becomes even more clear, because there is always, in fact, mutual dependence between superiors and subordinates. The plan that is born in the mind of the superior cannot be brought to fruition without the ready will of his subordinates, without some love, or without an eager, ready determination to meet halfway whatever has arisen in their chief's mind.

The most intelligent plan is not enough if there is no love in its performance. Subordinates must give their hearts to the plans, goals, and work of those over them, and not just to their persons.

Workers, in turn, will not be able to complete their tasks if they do not allow themselves to be directed. The superior depends, in his plans, not so much on his own orders as on the good will of his employees. This can even be seen in a dictatorship, for even the dictators during the late war often had to appeal to the good will of the workers. In work the will and the heart become closer to one another, and this becomes the test of the real value of the bonds of the group, the profession, the society, the company, and the assembly. There is a real coming together of one with the other, to the extent that everyone concerned is conscious of the mutual exchange of services.

Cooperation calls for education and love

In practicing cooperation we should always make use of the principle: first teach and then give orders and make demands. An educational — and not power-conscious — attitude should be expressed by every order, particularly in relation to beginners. The order must be clearly defined and the goal of the work should be pointed out.

The subordinates should also be ruled by this educational spirit, this will to learn in work. Through work a certain measure of perfection has to be fulfilled. For one of the aims of every sort of work is the perfecting of the workers. Listening to the instructions of our superiors, we should have the desire to accept those directions in a proper spirit, and the intention of making use of the work given us to derive new spiritual values from it. Work then will not be a hardship, but rather a school in which by obeying orders, we shall train our will and intellect continuously. Every type of work ought to form and cultivate something in us.

And the second very important factor in cooperation is the following one: we should remember that in every sort of work man meets with man, and so the relationship must be personal, which means that it must bind together persons and not things or affairs. Persons at work have the priority here; affairs or things only take second place.

It is only when individuals at work are linked by the chain of love, when love embraces their mutual relations, that work yields its full fruit. For as regards material things or business matters, the important thing is justice, which gives to everyone what belongs to him. Our method of proceeding should be such that we never sacrifice people to things, that the conduct of our various affairs never harms the human personality, which is the highest and most important good in these affairs.

When we confront the differences arising from human weakness, we should act according to the proven principle: *Suaviter in modo, fortiter in re*, "gently but firmly." We may not carry over the right relationship toward things into our dealings with people. Even when an affair or an object demands peremptoriness, the human being always has the right to love.

If we have to give or to hear criticism or reproof for work done poorly, we must not take it personally. If a reprimand is necessary, we should not think that our superiors like us less: a reprimand in work usually relates to things, while the attitude to the individual remains the same. Certainly, superiors have the right to see to it that the work is done well; they have the right to be firm; but in exercising this right they retain their love of our souls and our good. Love blunts the sharpness of the necessary stricture, criticism, or punishment.

One further remark: in cooperation we must always keep before our eyes our brothers and neighbors at work. In every injunction and command, superiors and subordinates are bound by the bonds of brotherhood. Our behavior as regards our neighbors must therefore be based not so much on our will as on our heart. The Christian love of one's neighbor says here that when it comes to giving orders, it is not what *I* want but what the human heart can endure that must be the measure of the relationship. By applying this principle we ensure that every order will be just and related to human capacity. This leads to a subtle insight into human capabilities; it gives the person who is receiving the orders the certainty that his superiors are taking human powers of endurance into consideration, and that they regard the working man as a living being. As a result, the hardest order will be sweetened and will be accepted in the spirit in which it is given.

In all cooperation with difficult people we give proof of our love for God; we know that we have this love if we can live and work with others. There is no great art in being able to work with easy people. When working with those who are difficult we have to guard against prejudice, against such feelings as "it would be impossible to cooperate with *them*." If we succeed in establishing relations with difficult people, in conquering their resistance with love, we can win over our brothers both for ourselves and for God.

20

Time for Work and Time for Rest

Every sort of work leads to realization, to completion. Completion means rest. So all work leads to some rest.

In connection with this truth we notice two tendencies at present. On the one hand, we observe the myth of work, the fever, the deification of work, the attempt to raise it to the highest dignity, to a virtue, to sanctity almost. This tendency and its accompanying propaganda have brought about a state of affairs where man is so schooled in continual effort that he is almost afraid of rest. Workers, grown unaccustomed to a day of rest because their employers so often exploited them, do not know what to do with a day off, and actually feel ill at ease. The long-standing compulsion to work has increased to such a degree that it has taken from man his longing for rest and created in him a fever of external activity.

This is one trend: the drive to get the greatest possible output, "the record" — that new motto for workers.

The second tendency, which runs parallel to the first, is the arrangement of life so that man may work as short a time as possible — two, three, five hours only — so as to free him from work and replace him by a machine.

God's thought long ago reconciled and solved both these tendencies by the divine law: "Six days shalt thou labor, and shalt do all thy works. But the seventh day is the Sabbath of the Lord."[156]

A rest! That is to say, a break in work, a holy rest directed toward the Lord. And therefore this rest should have certain religious features.

Let us look at the general conditions that must serve as a basis for this repose. Let us first of all consider the problem from the point of view of the working man, in order that we may later discuss the connection between the temporal rest and the religious character of the feast day. God's commandment tells us that work is man's duty, but it is not his most important duty. For there is a greater one: the Sabbath of the Lord. This demonstrates that work is a means for the development and perfecting of man, but not the most important means.

Here a question arises: how does one reconcile the wish to work with the need for rest? Where is the borderline between zeal in work and moderation in rest?

Work has its daily burden, its daily difficulty, and daily task; but it also has its holy week of work, its burden of a whole lifetime. Let us look at these three stages of human life.

The workday must achieve two goals

It is possible to limit the duration of work according to the goal of our daily toil. What is this goal?

Daily work should be of such a kind as to ensure the greatest material and economic efficiency and to justify man's right to a fair

[156]Exod. 20:9-10.

wage. In short, there must be a result, the concrete value of this work. And this is the first task of the day. In our examination of conscience we must ask ourselves the question: "What is the actual result that I have to show, what is the sum of this day's work, which will justify my right to my bread?" "The laborer is worthy of his hire," Christ will say.[157] This is the fruit of work, justice in the purely temporal order, in the name of which we can say, "Give us this day our daily bread."

And the second task of the day? Today's work ought to be such as to contribute to the normal development of man's abilities and personal powers. Why? Because man must strive continually to perfect his powers of reason and will, from which he cannot take a vacation. It is necessary that there be continuity in the work of our spiritual powers.

We are faced with the eternal question: What did I achieve as a result of the day's work in terms of the development of my mental powers and the perfecting of my will? Now, just as work perfects, so also the lack of it demoralizes the mind and weakens the will. The working day must help the progress of our mind and will.

The day's work should be such that it does not exhaust all our human powers. A man ending a day's work should still have some physical strength at his disposal.

Prudence and justice command man to refrain from the sort of work that would exhaust his strength completely, for work is not the most important task; it is not the only duty in the day, or in life, either.

The day's work should be of such a kind that one is able, with the strength left over, to fulfil the other daily tasks of life. A man coming from work should still have the wish and the energy to work at other things. He should still have some time, as well as

[157]Luke 10:7.

physical and spiritual strength. *Rerum Novarum* defines this in the following manner: "Daily labor, therefore, must be so regulated that it may not be protracted during longer hours than strength admits."[158] Work must make way for the other tasks of the day. Man must have time for prayer, for rest, for conversation with his family, for his hobbies, and for helping his neighbor. When work is over man must remain a man, that is to say, a social being.

The workday must be neither too long nor too short

Then there is the problem as to which is better, a longer or a shorter working day. This depends to a great extent on the qualities of the working man, on his ability, talents, and strength. It is clear that these are unequally divided. For man to be able to perform all his tasks, the working day should neither be too short nor too long. Both those who want the longest possible working day and those who incline to only three or four hours of work a day are making a mistake.

Why should the working day not be too short? Principally because man needs a certain amount of concentration in his work. His energies need to develop gradually, and time is needed for this.

It is not easy to achieve concentration in work. Every work is difficult in the beginning. With short hours of work the losses by way of preparation and lack of concentration are too great. For this reason also, too frequent changes in work are not desirable, because, economically speaking, they are not at all useful, for too much scattering of energy and attention is involved. The mere settling down to work takes time. Therefore, wherever work is well organized, too frequent changes are avoided out of consideration

[158] Leo XIII, *Rerum Novarum*. English translation in *Four Great Encyclicals*, 24.

for the psychological well-being of the worker. This likewise demands special supervision, for although it is a fact that there are people capable of applying themselves to every sort of work, this only occurs rarely.

But the working day ought not to be too long either, for human work is efficient, useful, and joyous only if it is really to man's liking and does not exceed his strength and capabilities. This is the problem of the ideal working hours that would ensure the usefulness of the work. Their number can fluctuate considerably; we must therefore find out what is correct.

Daily experience teaches us that if work is too long, strength is exhausted, the rate of work is slackened, and eagerness diminishes, as does the effectiveness and value of the work. We must also take into account moral considerations, for man's moral responsibility only goes so far. Beyond that point, moral disorganization sets in. The organizers of work are responsible for this if they are indifferent to the actual possibilities beyond which a man begins to work on sheer nervous energy and not in the spirit in which God wishes him to work.

Work that is too long and that exceeds man's allowance of perseverance, can become harmful and hateful. It injures the worker himself from the moral, psychological, and physical point of view, for it wears away his strength. It injures the very object of work, for in such a state of affairs one does not work conscientiously. It also injures society, for people who are overtired are usually bitter, sad, downhearted, hard to please, and do not have normal reactions. It is difficult to deal successfully with such people, or to arouse enthusiasm in them.

The duration of work cannot be determined by economic factors alone, because these factors do not constitute the highest human good. It is true that a man should work so as to fulfil his responsibility, in cooperation with God, to feed the world and thus increase the supply of economic goods and, in so doing, fulfil his moral obligations. But at the same time, he must work in such a way that he does not waste his physical and spiritual strength prematurely and turn into some sort of robot, but is able to fulfil his obligations as the head or member of a family, a nation, society, profession, or country.

When he leaves his work, a man must, again, be able to take part in religious life, and in prayer; he must have the opportunity and the wish to draw on spiritual gifts in order to worship God both in public and in private. People sometimes give as their excuse for not going to church that Sunday is the only day left to them for their personal affairs — to get something washed, to sew and, above all, to sleep more. If sleep becomes man's ideal, it means that there is something wrong with his work.

Excessive work crowds out other obligations

How should work appear in relation to the tasks of human life as a whole?

In the final analysis, even when human strength is husbanded, it wears out irreparably. The night's rest does, indeed, renew our strength. Sunday invigorates us for the coming week. But there comes a time when a night, a weekend, a holiday, or a stay in a health resort cannot help any more. "For all our days are spent; and in Thy wrath we have fainted away. . . . The years of our life are threescore and ten years, or even by reason of strength fourscore; yet their span is but toil and trouble."[159] Age, sickness, unfortunate events in our life and in work itself: all these things take their toll.

God gave man strength for the performance of life's tasks in their entirety. To arrive at perfection, a long span of life is usually

[159]Ps. 89:9-10 (RSV = Ps. 90:9-10).

necessary. This is why, with certain exceptions, human life lasts a long time.

Work should not burn up human life too early, for man would then not be able to fulfil all the tasks of his life. People are inclined to neglect their duties to God and their souls; it is the interior life that is most threatened by excess of work.

Moreover, the skill that man acquires in work only comes with the years. A young man just beginning work usually spoils his material at first. It is only when he is older that he attains a certain amount of experience, which raises both the value of the man and of his work. The experienced worker is usually elderly. It is necessary, therefore, to wait for ripeness of years.

Work that is too exhausting physically makes it impossible for us to acquire moral virtues and perfections. This catchphrase, "the greatest possible output of work," has shown that man, working in accordance with this motto, will be a good worker for a certain while but will then become incapable of any of the other tasks of life. Social workers have arrived at the conclusion that overworked people are not fit for social activity. Nor are they capable of developing within themselves many of the human virtues.

It sometimes happens that the more that physical strength is used, the more feebly life develops in other ways and the less progress is made in spiritual work. From this originates the one-sidedness of a certain human type, which may be noticed especially in proletarian or peasant environments.

Such a man can ask, "For what profit shall a man have of all his labor and vexation of spirit, with which he hath been tormented under the sun?"[160]

It is very easy for overworked people to become materialists. Poets can write so beautifully of times of work in nature's bosom,

[160]Eccles. 2:22.

while the actual workers do not even see the nature that surrounds them. They do not have time to wonder at its beauty. They do not see the charm of the mountains, the sunset, or the miracles of vegetation. Sometimes mountain dwellers are shocked when they hear townsfolk admiring these "rocks." Theirs is usually a utilitarian and material attitude to nature, and this is the result of too one-sided, too heavy work. It is necessary therefore to conserve man's strength for life's tasks as a whole.

Once upon a time there were longer rests in work. The *Angelus* set a limit to evening work. No one dared work longer in the field. In the same way in the Old Testament they only worked until sunset. On the vigils of feasts, devotions ended the working day — this was the old "English Sabbath." Artisans, apprentices, and masters all used to come to these devotions, for this was their service. There were also longer holidays in connection with periodic feasts such as Easter and Pentecost. These workers' holidays, which are so extolled today, were for centuries supported by the Church by means of feasts lasting several days, which took one away from the burden of work. Here and there artisans kept the custom of stopping their work from Easter Sunday until the following Sunday.

Today the feasts and the customs connected with them are disappearing. But it is necessary to defend them, for they are the deliverance of human life.

Concentration helps us to work more efficiently

But what is one to do when there is too much work? How does one increase time, when God made the day too short and the night too long? This is the problem to be solved.

Its solution lies rather in man's inner attitude. On him depends the place that the time for work takes in the scheme of things. It is a question of the formation of our inner psychological attitude to work. We must say to ourselves, "Do what you are doing." It is necessary to avoid scattering or overlapping our activities; our deeds must be "full before God."[161] This is the command that calls for concentration in work.

Work is often inefficient because we do not possess the art of concentrating on our work; we lack order in our thoughts and in our performance. We must therefore intensify our inner efficiency. Much evil and waste of time flow from inner disorder. That is why we are commanded to avoid inner division and the dispersal of our thoughts. The problem of "lack of time" is not to be solved by haste, but by calm. We must acquire calmness in work. Diffuse haste only increases work. We must begin by putting in order our inner spiritual attitude.

But organization on the material side (that is, our method of planning work to increase our amount of time) is also important. This is where the directors of work come into their own.

This is the background against which we arrive at a better understanding of God's commandment: "Six days shalt thou labor, and shalt do all thy works. But the seventh day is the Sabbath of the Lord."

[161] Cf. Rev. 3:2.

21

Sunday

We read the following in the book of Genesis, in the final verses describing creation: "So the heavens and the earth were finished, and all the host of them. And on the seventh day God ended His work which He had made; and He rested on the seventh day from all His work which He had done. And He blessed the seventh day, and sanctified it, because in it He had rested from all His work which He had created and made."[162]

From the moment this blessing was linked with rest from labor, the seventh day has had a double task in the history of God's world: the giving of worship to God and the granting of rest to the tired body and mind.

Holy days of rest are essential to human life

Every type of work is a link that binds us to the created world, to our neighbors, and to God. By means of this bond of friendship

[162]Gen. 2:1-3.

our work is changed into prayer. It is not enough for the human heart to devote the whole day or even six days of the week to binding sheaves: for it to be fully satisfied there must be a possibility, either in the evening or at the end of the toilsome week, for him to offer his sheaves to God. And so work for six days always prepares for the seventh day of the Lord.

Holy days are "the voice of one crying in the wilderness: make straight the way of the Lord."[163] They remind us to pay homage to God, the Father of all creation, of life, and of grace; to tear ourselves away from matter, to free ourselves from its powerful influence, to realize that it is not creation that governs man but man creation, to remember the service of God, which is the most wonderful and fitting thing we can do, to come to Him through our own sanctification, and to become like God. All this is the special task of the feast day.

All these tasks have to be put within man's reach by a day that is free from ordinary, everyday work. For religious life, the fulfilment of one's duties toward God, and the fulfilment of the needs of the mind and the heart, are the main aims of freedom from work, a freedom that should do good to both soul and body. For the rest on Sunday or a feast day does not mean unproductive idleness but is "rest from labor, consecrated by religion. Repose united with religious observance disposes man to forget for a while the business of this daily life, and to turn his thought to heavenly things and to the worship which he so strictly owes to the Eternal Deity."[164]

Sundays and holy days are meant to remind us that, in addition to temporal work, there are other labors in the vineyard of our own soul. And we should always be mindful of this truth, especially in

[163] Isa. 40:3; Mark 1:3.

[164] Leo XIII, *Rerum Novarum*. English translation in *Four Great Encyclicals*, 23.

view of the fairly frequent attempts to rob these holy days of their religious character.

Through the sanctification of the seventh day the human right to rest was surrounded with a wall of inviolability. Wherever God's commandment "Remember thou keep holy the Sabbath day" has disappeared, wherever war has been declared on religion, there is an immediate increase in the burden of human work, the crushing load of toil from the cradle to the grave.

Whoever violates the holy day is working most effectively to his own disadvantage, by his very advocacy of the abolition of days of rest. Today's violation of the holy day is tomorrow's violation of the right of man to honest leisure. The worker is protected by his right to a holy day against this temptation to exploit his strength beyond its possibilities.

The violation of the human right to look for God is reflected in the increased sense of the burden of work, in disillusionment with life, in the disappearance of interest, in indifference to all other human duties, in depression, in an increasing sense of social degradation, in the growing sense of the hopelessness of existence, and in the spirit of opposition and revolt. There is no time for God, or for one's own children; there is only continuous work.

God gives us His own example of rest from work

Is it not touching, this example of God, whom nothing can weary, taking a rest? Behind the words, we can sense the real intention: to give us an example. God is the master not only of our soul but of our body as well, which is why He protects this creation of His hands, that it may not be worn-out too soon.

So, with God Himself as an example, man has "to rest" from the work of his hands in order to give relief to his body and a change to his spirit. Into the greyness of the days of work, into the hopelessness of an existence of continuous toil without change or break, the heavenly Father introduced the day of rest, relief, and joy. He also ordered His servant, the Church, to spare no effort to introduce into human life this divine precept as a social law, through the codes and enactments of state law. And what an effort it cost the Church to break down human resistance, before the world could be brought to recognize the law of rest from work as a social and cultural achievement!

Complete and effective rest after work is only possible in the religious atmosphere of a holy day. We can only know by experience the meaning the holy day has for rest after work. It is very significant that all the holidays and feasts that Moses introduced at God's command, combined two aims: the religious one, which was the glory of God, and the purely human one, which was rest.

Every sort of work tends ultimately to rest, to creating a moment when the worker, having satisfied all his needs, can learn in quiet and calmness that man does not live by bread alone. It is only by abandoning himself to this rest and meditating on his completed work that man comes face-to-face with God's infinite and holy energy. Here, in contact with God, in inward communion with Him, man becomes filled with love, a love that is poured forth in further work with holy prodigality. In this way our work rests in God, and in Him it launches out into fresh effort. In the quiet of rest "the God of our strength"[165] is born in us, and continually renews the youthfulness of our days.

The holy day rest must be communal and social

Besides its religious character, fruitful rest after work requires other conditions. First of all, this rest must be general. We are

[165]Cf. Ps. 42:2 (RSV = Ps. 43:2).

raised out of ourselves, and, at the same time, when we share in blissful relaxation and have around us a feeling of relief blessed by the peace of the God whom we adore, we are soothed by communal rest. Master and servant are closer to one another; for now that the marks of toil are obliterated, they resemble one another, and they meet in the presence of the common Father.

When all creation is included in this rest, and, without detriment to urgent matters, as many people as possible take part in it, there is a real "holy day" atmosphere, which adds to the value of the physical rest itself.

Rest after work must also be social. The whole human community, all together and on the same day, should worship God by communal prayer and by stopping work. It is only then, with our neighbors' joy before us, that our own happiness achieves its fullest expression in the love of God and of our brothers.

22

Joy in Work

From what do the joys of human work flow? God wanted man himself to be the creator of his own well-being. In depriving him of all ready-made instruments, God left him with the most precious gifts of all: reason and his hands. Here precisely is the source of all our joy in work. Thanks to our talents we have the possibility of continuous improvement, of changing the instruments of our work, and of spiritualizing the whole of human work, including every facet of it down to the lowest form of service. All honest work ends, even after the hardest toil, with a certain joy.

Work can bring about natural joy

Different kinds of work are not hard or toilsome to the same extent. There are pleasant forms of work; and even in extremely exhausting work there can be sublime moments. For there exists some natural joy for man in triumphing in the act of making things that will serve human needs. There are types of work, especially those closer to nature, which contain much human joy. The farmer beams at the sight of growing corn, an abundant crop, and trees full of beautiful fruit.

Do we not feel joy in the very act of using our energy, our abilities, our physical and spiritual faculties? Let us look at the healthy, smiling, sunburned faces (even if they are sometimes moist with sweat) of people who know the value of useful creative effort. In such physical labor, man takes delight.

But we are faced with something still more profound: our consciousness of self. Thus we are faced not only with the satisfaction that comes from our inborn skill in work, but also with the sense of our own personality, which is reflected in our works and somehow projects us into them. Man feels an almost divine joy when he contemplates the signs of his labor in material works. Just as God during the seven days of creation declared repeatedly that all He had made was very good, so man in his works sees a reflection of his own image.

How often we recognize the master from his work: the artist, scientist, artisan, and farmer from the fruits of their work! These works indeed bear witness to the man. When we want to know the worth of a man, we ask what he does and what he has achieved.

Man sees in his work the continual development of his abilities and qualities. He sees the development of his personality, as well as his growing physical and spiritual powers, to which increasingly perfect works bear witness. Does not this make us happy? In this happiness man completely forgets the pain and labor of work. If he does remember the toil or how he overcame his difficulties, do not these memories afford new causes for joy? Besides, is it not just when we have managed to struggle through a whole forest of sufferings and trials that our well-wishers express their admiration and respect for us?

When our work is already crowned with success, when our efforts — of many years, perhaps — have brought us to our goal, which is the liberation of man by the fulfilment of his longings, how much joy this gives us! In this happy state of exaltation, plans for new work usually arise, although we know beforehand that they will once more wring sweat from our brows, "the burden of the day and the heat,"[166] grief, pain, and sleepless nights. Our joy rises above all this; the man who gives himself over to idleness will never know it.

Nor will the man who does not know how tiring work can be ever know real rest. Even when it comes to amusing himself, it is only the working man who can have full pleasure.

And finally, there is the joy that flows from the feeling of having completed some task that will be useful for one's neighbors. Man is glad that he has given some preconceived form to matter, that he has made something in his own image and likeness, and that through this both he and his work are of service and have achieved human usefulness. When we consider the work itself, its goodness, usefulness, fitness, and its acceptance by other people, joy is born in us, as well as love for the work of our hands, which is similar to the love of God for the world.

Was Ecclesiastes not right: "And I have known that there was no better thing than to rejoice, and do well in this life"?[167]

Work can bring about supernatural joy

For human work is love for God and for one's brother. It is the reply of a rational being to the summons of love by which God asked us in a sublime manner to cooperate in His creative activity. Man plays the part of the second cause in the government, by Providence, of the world.

[166]Matt. 20:12.
[167]Eccles. 3:12.

From this derives the great dignity of man working with God and also the unusual dignity of his work: it is cooperation between man and God in both joys and sorrows. It is the work of prayer, worship, and the love of God.

As such, work becomes for man the source of great new joy from the vocation and elevation by which he has been honored, from the knowledge that he is acting "hand in hand" with the Creator, from the graces of his state flowing over all his works, and from the actual grace given like a good spirit to all his efforts, labors, and works.

A new joy flows from love for men. St. Paul bears witness to how necessary this love is in work: "I may give away all that I have, to feed the poor; I may give myself up to be burnt at the stake; but if I lack charity, it goes for nothing."[168]

How many people burn themselves out at work! There is no lack either of people who, while proclaiming the dignity of work, look on it with hatred as a sad necessity. This is an almost universal tragedy, just as work is a universal phenomenon.

And yet work has its usual reward in the love of men and the world. Through work a link is forged with other people, and this teaches us to love. Man works so as to create and renew the good things that are useful to his neighbors; the fruit of our work is the proof of our friendliness to other people. In this sense, work brings us closer to love of our neighbors in God. And therefore work cannot be carried out with a clenched fist and a shrivelled heart. The heart must unfold just as the hand must. Otherwise it is not real work. It is only at this price that the hardest work, like charity, "sustains, believes, hopes, and endures to the last."[169] It is only then that the heaviest sacrifices that go with work can be faced

[168] 1 Cor. 13:3.
[169] 1 Cor. 13:7.

without class hatred, only then that work gives out all those virtues without which it cannot be fruitful. "Charity is patient, is kind, feels no envy, is never perverse or proud, never insolent, does not claim its rights, cannot be provoked, does not brood over an injury; . . . but rejoices at the victory of truth."[170] Of truth! Of this truth: that all creation is filled by the open hands of people, as by the open hands of God, with a plenitude of blessings.

And there is one more human joy in work, a joy that is really divine. This is the joy that comes from the fact that work done with love helps to achieve man's redemption. When we unite our work with an act of love for God, by this love we lighten our labor; we wipe the sweat from our brows.

When we undertake work from love of God, this merciful God lets us share in a task of great honor and efficacy — that of atonement. Thus it follows that work in the sweat of our brow both cleanses and ennobles us. The feeling of freedom that work gives is the highest joy. To gaze at God, face-to-face, gladdens us through all our toil and weariness. Our sorrow is turned into joy.

[170] 1 Cor. 13:4-6.

Biographical Note

Stefan Cardinal Wyszynski

"An indefatigable pastor and indomitable witness of the Gospel of Christ."

Pope John Paul II

Stefan Cardinal Wyszynski, head of the Roman Catholic Church in Poland for thirty-two years, was a commanding figure who combined the skills of a diplomat, politician, and spiritual leader. Under his authority, the Polish church became the strongest independent social force in Eastern Europe, a natural focus of opposition to the Communist state, and an indispensable source of support for the burgeoning independent labor movement *Solidarity*, which was led by the Cardinal's friend, Lech Walesa. Subsequent to Cardinal Wyszynski's death, *Solidarity* was instrumental in toppling the Communist government and Lech Walesa was elected President of Poland.

Nor has Cardinal Wyszynski's influence been limited to Poland. Karol Wojtyla, his student, friend, and fellow Cardinal, was elected Pope in 1978. Just days after his elevation to the papacy, John Paul II publicly praised his mentor, Cardinal Wyszynski, telling him, "I would not be here today if it were not for your faith (unwavering even in the face of suffering and imprisonment) and for your heroic hope, and if there were not the whole period in the history of our country which is associated with your episcopal and primatial service." Through his student and friend John Paul II, the influence of Stefan Cardinal Wyszynski has spread throughout the world.

Stefan Wyszynski was born August 3, 1901, in a section of eastern Poland that was then part of Russia. He was ordained a priest in 1924, and afterward undertook doctoral studies in sociology and canon law at the Catholic University in Lublin. While a student, he became interested in Catholic social doctrine and its application, an interest that continued throughout his life. In the 1930s Wyszynski taught in a Catholic seminary and was active in Christian trade movements. During this time, he also wrote numerous scholarly articles and books. During World War II, he supported the Polish resistance movement against the German occupation and served as chaplain for the underground Polish Home Army. He was elected bishop of Lublin in 1946 and then primate of Poland in 1949.

Shortly before the Cardinal was elevated to the primacy, the Communist party gained control of the Polish government and set out to destroy the Catholic Church in Poland with a series of repressive measures against the clergy and the laity. At first seeking a *modus vivendi* with the government, Cardinal Wyszynski was increasingly forced to denounce the government's violation of the rights of the people and its efforts to destroy religion in Poland. Relations between Church and state deteriorated. Finally, in the autumn of 1953, the Polish secret police arrested the Cardinal, imprisoning him for three years in a series of monasteries.

Although a change of regime in 1956 allowed Father Wyszynski to be released, for the rest of his life he vigorously asserted the rights of the Polish people to practice their Catholic faith despite the continued harassment of the Communist government. In this period, he also became an important mediator between the state and workers' groups pressing for reform. In particular, he had a significant influence in the 1970s on the independent labor organization *Solidarity* and its leader, Lech Walesa, who was then a frequent visitor to the Cardinal's residence and is now the President of Poland.

The Cardinal's wise and moderating influence on all segments of Polish society prevented the dangerous political unrest that could have led to a Soviet takeover and the loss of Polish independence in the postwar period.

Upon his death on May 28, 1981, eloquent testimony to Cardinal Wyszynski's central role in the history of modern Poland was given by all of the Polish people — from Communist leaders to militant trade unionists — who joined in observing a four-day period of mourning for him. His funeral Mass drew some three hundred thousand Poles, and the Polish regime, which once had branded him as one of the "greatest foes of the Polish People's Republic," accorded him full state honors at his burial.

A highly educated intellectual who yet knew how to communicate with any audience in everyday terms, a passionate patriot but an even more passionate servant of the Faith, Stefan Cardinal Wyszynski was a remarkable man whose devotion to Christ and His Mystical Body was perfectly summed up in the motto on his personal coat of arms: *Soli Deo*, "for God alone."

Sophia Institute Press®

Sophia Institute Press is a nonprofit institution that seeks to restore man's knowledge of eternal truth, including man's knowledge of his own nature, his relation to other persons, and his relation to God.

Sophia Institute Press® serves this end in numerous ways: by publishing translations of foreign works to make them accessible for the first time to English-speaking readers; by bringing back into print books that have been long out of print; and by publishing important new books that fulfill the ideals of Sophia Institute. These books afford readers a rich source of the enduring wisdom of mankind.

Sophia Institute Press® makes these high-quality books available to the general public by using advanced technology and by soliciting donations to subsidize its general publishing costs.

Your generosity can help Sophia Institute Press® to provide the public with editions of works containing the enduring wisdom of the ages. Please send your tax-deductible contribution to the address below. The members of the Editorial Board of Sophia Institute Press® welcome questions, comments, and suggestions from all of our readers.

For your free catalog, call:

Toll-free: 1-800-888-9344

or write:

Sophia Institute Press®

Box 5284, Manchester, NH 03108

Internet users may visit our website at:

http://www.sophiainstitute.com

Sophia Institute is a tax-exempt institution
as defined by the Internal Revenue Code,
Section 501(c)(3). Tax I.D. 22-2548708.